Historic Landscapes
Summit County, Colorado
Ghost Towns and Townsites

Volume 2

Lincoln City

By

Bill Fountain
Sandra Mather, PhD

SUMMIT HISTORICAL SOCIETY PRESS

Published in the United States of American by Summit Historical Society Press, 103 LaBonte Street, P.O. Box 143 Dillon, Colorado 80435

www.summithistorical.org

Historic Landscapes, Summit County, Colorado,
Ghost Towns and Townsites,
Volume 2: Lincoln City

Authors: Bill Fountain and Sandra F. Mather, PhD
Editors: Bill Fountain and Sandra F. Mather, PhD

1st edition: April 1, 2024

ISBN: 978-1-943829-56-9

Library of Congress Control Number: 2024906781

Summit Historical Society Press is an imprint of Rhyolite Press LLC, P.O. Box 60144, Colorado Springs, CO 80960.

This book is sponsored by C.J. Mueller

Cover Photos:
Top: Buildings at the West End of Lincoln City, 1923

Bottom trio L to R:
     Wood Cut Engraving of Lincoln City, 1879 Mining Journal
     Lincoln City from Farncomb Hill, 1885
     Lincoln City, 1923

Book Design & Layout: Marla Morelos

DEDICATION

For many years, a group of people working individually and collaboratively has investigated, documented, and interpreted the historic landscapes of Breckenridge and Summit County — collecting photographs, documents, and artifacts for the benefit of future generations; writing books, monographs, and newspaper articles; leading field experiences; presenting special programs; and sharing their expertise willingly whenever asked.

Larry Crispell, Mary Ellen Gilliland, Leigh Girvin, Rick Hague, Kris Ann Knish, Maureen Nicholls, Larissa O'Neil, Bob Schoppe, Rich Skovlin, Robin Theobald, Eric Twitty, Wendy Wolfe—to you we dedicate this series of books and say thank you and Mahalo.

TABLE OF CONTENTS

Acknowledgments 6

Prologue 7

Lincoln City 9

Bibliography 112

Index 114

About the Authors 116

ACKNOWLEDGMENTS

As with any publication, certain individuals, governmental agencies, and other entities provided vital assistance, support, and encouragement. A big thank you goes to Maureen Nicholls, Robin Theobald, Ed and Nancy (deceased) Bathke, Rich Skovlin, Rick Hague, *Colorado Postal Historian*, the Summit Historical Society, Summit County Clerk and Recorder's Office, and the Bureau of Land Management in Lakewood, Colorado.

Much of the research comes from the Colorado Historic Newspaper Collection website (www.coloradohistoricnewspapers.org). The *Summit County Journal*, the *Breckenridge Bulletin*, and the *Summit County Journal and Breckenridge Bulletin* (The two merged for almost five years beginning in October, 1909.) are available online from 1892 until early 1923.

We extend heartfelt gratitude to Eric Twitty, owner of Mountain States Historical, for granting us special permission to quote and use maps from his Colorado Cultural Resource Survey. His research and writing truly enhanced the quality of our manuscript.

The aerial photographs at the end of the chapters came from Google Earth.

A very special thank you to Mike Shipley, CEO of Key Media, who offered the services of his company in laying out not only this book but all seven in this series. Mike owns the Country Boy Mine in French Gulch near Breckenridge, which draws tourists and residents alike to experience an authentic late 1800s mine. Mike also supported the publication of the book, *Country Boy Mine, Breckenridge, Colorado, 1881 – 1994*, by Fountain and Mather.

Also, many thanks to Marla Morelos, Head of Graphic Design for Key Media, for preparing the layout. She has become a treasured colleague.

PROLOGUE

Why *Historic Landscapes, Summit County, Colorado*? Bill Fountain explains: My idea of writing a book about the historic towns of Summit County found from Hoosier Pass north to the confluence of the Blue and Swan rivers and from the Ten Mile Range east to the historic towns of Rexford and Swandyke originated in spring, 2021.

Using information taken from first-hand accounts such as the mining district logbooks from 1859 and early 1860 and newspaper articles written by those who had observed and reported what they saw and then personally exploring the sites, alone and with others, I mentally traveled back in time imagining life at those locations over 150 years ago. I hope readers will do the same as they read the books in this series.

The *Chasing the Dream* series told the stories of Parkville, Rexford, Swandyke, Wapiti, Valdora, and Tonopah Camp 2. This series will include abbreviated versions of their history.

As I started identifying all the historic sites within my chosen boundaries, I decided to include railroad stations, even though some of them were not truly townsites. I selected 27 sites—some relatively unknown; some known by a few. About most, little had been written.

It soon became apparent that the "book" I envisioned would exceed 1,000 pages of text, documents, and maps—and that didn't count the more than 1,050 figures/photographs I wanted to include.

After discussions with my co-author and others, I concluded that a series of books made more sense. Sandie suggested the title, *Historic Landscapes, Summit County, Colorado*. We divided the sites into two categories: ghost towns and townsites with five books; and railroad stations and sites with two books. Will we expand the boundaries of the research leading to more books? Perhaps.

Figure PR-1 includes the location of all the ghost towns, historic townsites, and train stations found in *Historic Landscapes, Summit County, Colorado*.

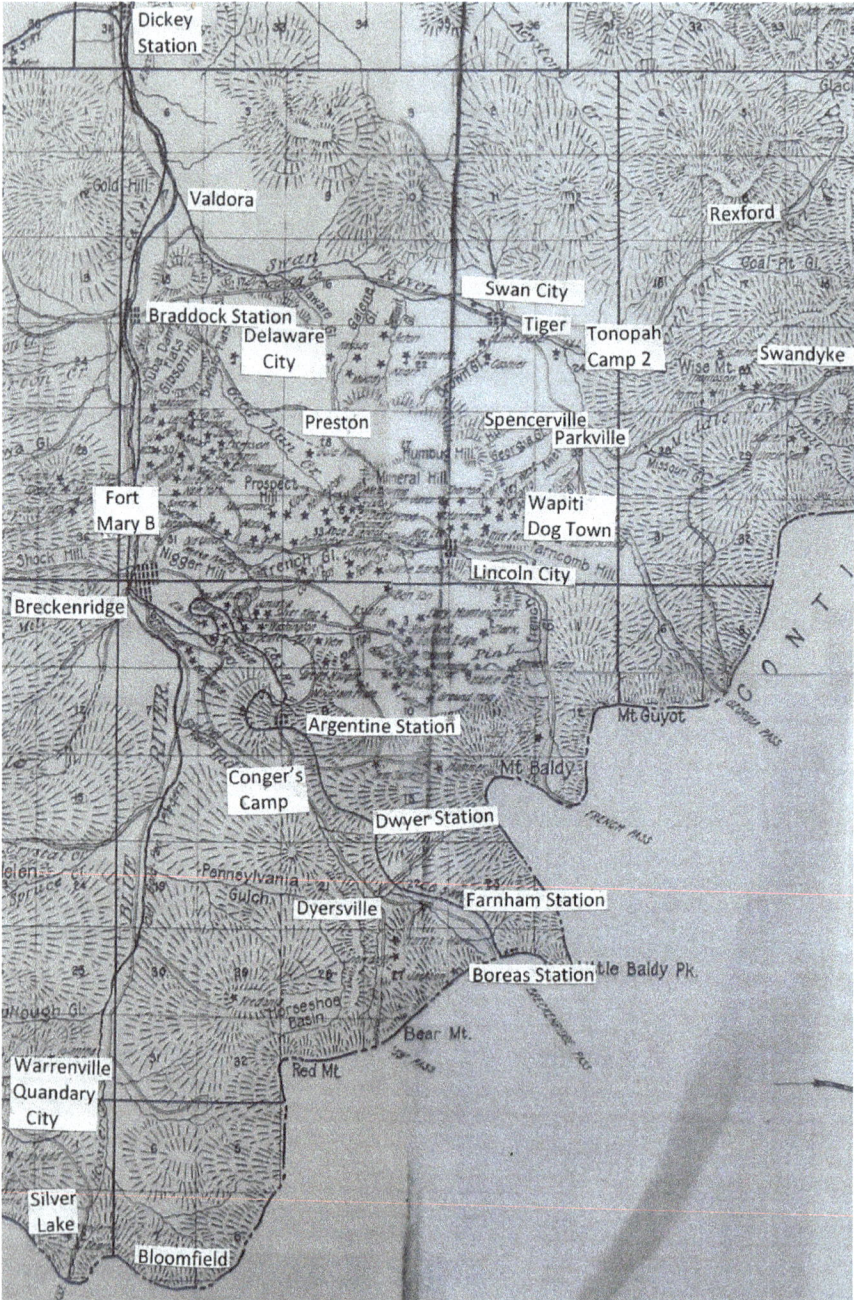

Figure PR-1. Map of a Portion of Summit County showing Ghost Towns, Historic Townsites, and Train Stations. (Author's Collection)

LINCOLN CITY

Lincoln City Townsite Location

L incoln City can be found east of Breckenridge in French Gulch, a short distance west of the intersection of Sallie Barber Road and French Gulch Road. The earliest known photograph of Lincoln City appears in **Figure 1**; the map in **Figure 2** shows the location of this true ghost town.

Because the merchants of Lincoln City provided the goods and services required by those living in the eastern section of French Gulch, this chapter will focus on the mining activity in the gulch.

Early History of French Gulch

Although the first documented discovery of gold in the Blue River occurred on August 10, 1859, other discoveries including those in French Gulch happened as early as the spring of 1859.

Figure 1. The Earliest Known Photograph of Lincoln City, 1860s. (Courtesy Maureen Nicholls)

Figure 2. Portion of an 1865 Frederick J. Ebert Map of Colorado Territory showing Lincoln. The word "City" has been dropped from the name. The map also includes Breckenridge and Parkville. (Author's Collection)

E.D.C., in the *Leadville Weekly Herald*, explained the French Creek name: "Late in the fall [1859] a Frenchman made a discovery on what is now known as French creek, from which he took an ounce of gold a day by the 'Long Tom' process. From this date the more important discoveries made in the tributary gulches of French and Illinois creeks, which followed each other in quick succession . . ." (May 1, 1880)

Although less traveled than Breckenridge, Georgia, and Hoosier passes, French Pass provided a popular way over the continental divide from South Park to Middle Park. The 1907 map in **Figure 3** shows French Pass (lower, right); South Park as a blank area; the road from Lincoln (City) to Breckenridge; and many large mines in French Gulch.

Merchants demanded roads. A toll road carried goods and people from South Park, over French Pass, to Lincoln City, a distance of 14 miles. (*The Fairplay Flume*, January 15, 1880)

"The county road up French gulch, through Lincoln City and over French pass, comes into South Park a short distance west of the old town of Jefferson . . ." (*Leadville Weekly Herald*, January 31, 1880)

As many as ten roads, including the one over French Pass, crossed the continental divide leading to and from Summit County:

"We have the wagon road over French pass, 11 miles northeast of Breckenridge, elevation about 11,800 feet. The pass is between Mount Baldy (or Mount Hamilton) on the west and Mount Guyot on the east, and we have also the Georgia pass, to the east of Mount Guyot, elevation about 11,800 feet. Both of these passes enter Summit county from South Park or Park county, and the distance from Denver to Breckenridge, via. Morrison, the upper part of South park and French pass is 90 miles, via. Georgia pass, 100 miles, or via. Colorado Springs, South Park and French pass, 146 miles. These roads are traveled very little by light vehicles and are not available, but can be put in good condition and easy grades. The French pass road follows French gulch from the said 'pass' to Breckenridge . . ." (*Summit County Journal & Breckenridge Bulletin*, January 10, 1913)

Figure 3. Portion of a 1907 Cramer Map showing French Pass. (Author's Collection)

On September 28, 2008, Fountain and Rick Hague drove to the end of French Creek Road and hiked the gentle path up to French Pass. Although they did not investigate the Park County side of the pass, they concluded that French Pass would have been an easier pass to negotiate than some of the others.

A New Mining District

Prospectors lined the creek. The *Rocky Mountain News* boasted on October 20, 1859, that "French Gulch is paying from ten to twelve dollars a day to the man"—indeed, excellent pay when most considered three dollars per day an excellent wage.

Miners quickly formed a mining district in 1859. Because the original logbook has disappeared, the name or date of formation cannot be determined.

Figure 4. The Approach to French Pass from the Summit County Side, 2008. (Photograph by Author)

The miners received permission to refile their claims in the Spaulding Mining District that included mines at the conjunction of French Creek and the Blue River. These filings from the Spaulding Mining District appear exactly as written in the logbook.

"Spaulding Destrict Record
On the French Gulch

This Article of agreement made and entered into this 25th day of September A D 1859 by and between Federick Kershaw Calvin Grey and Eugene Morgan Witnesseth that they the said Kershaw Grey and Morgan have this day Entered into a special Copartnership for the purpose of holding and working mining Claims within the Limits of the Spaulding Destrict but more particularly the Claims now owned by them on the French Gulch said claims being the ones severally known at the Discovery Claims and Claims Nos one and two below Dis and one and two above said discovery claims and also the Bank Claims Nos one two and three being above and adjoining the Creek claims above mentined said parties owning an Equal and undivided interest in all of the above mentioned claims it being the understanding that each of the Parties shall bear an Equal share of the Expences attending the working said claims and receive an Equal proportion of the procedes therefrom provideing it is mutually understood and agree by all parties that in consideration of said Kershaw relinqushing his interest in the Earnings from said claims during the present mineing season he shall be released from all costs and labor attending to the operations of the other parties on said claims during the period above mentioned and the said Grey and Morgan shall have the priviledge of running one sluice or Tom on either of the Companys claims in any was or manner they many see fit and be entitled to all the procedes thereof during the present mining season it is also understood and agreed that neither party shall have any right to dispose of his interest or of either of the others partys interest without the consent in writing of all parties being first obtained and should either party in violation of this agreement make sale of such interest it shall be null and void in witness inhereof we hereunto set our hands and affix our seals this 25th day of Sept A D 1859

In presence of)	Fred K Kershaw
J P McIntyre)	Calvin Grey
Joseph Cook)	Eugen Morgan

I herby certify that the above is a true copy of the original instrument

John. G. Randall

Secretary P

Know all men by these presents that I J. M. Francher did on the 25th day of August 1859 claim four claims situated in the Spaulding Destrick on the French Gulch and Discribed as follows claims No 2-3-4 and 5 above discovery claim and by these presents do claim said claims to have and to hold the same for mining purposes

I hereby certify that the above Record was made on the 22nd day of Oct 1859 at the Request of J. M. Francher in Person

John. G. Randall

Secretary P

Know all men by these presents that I E. N Tuttle did on the 22nd day of October 1859 claim one claim situated in the Spaulding Destrict on the French Gulch and known and Disignated as claim No 28 and by these presents do claim said claim to have and to hold the same for mining purposes

I hereby certify that the above Record was made on the 22nd day of Oct 1859 at the Request of J. M. Francher

John. G. Randall

Secretary

Know all men by these presents that We T B Turner O Nelson Brainard Nelson A Anderson O Nelson M Robinson Daniel Woodman Oscar F. Eddy and Thomas Bridge did on the 16th Day of October 1859 claim these claims situated in the Spaulding Destrict on the French Gulch and known and Designated as claims No 6 & 7 above Discovery claim and No 3 Below Discovery and after on the 21st day of Oct 1859 claimed two claims being Nos 4 & 5 Below Discovery and after on the 28th Day of Oct 1859 claimed two claims being Nos 8 & 9 above Discovery and on the same day claimed one claim being No 6 below Discovery and on the same day claimed one claim being claim No 10 above Discovery All of the above claims being situated on the French gulch in the Spaulding District and by these presents do claim said claims to have and to hold the service for mineing purposes

I hereby Certify that the above Record was made on the 28th day of Oct 1859 at the Requst of H. B. Turner

John. G. Randall

Secretary P

Know all men by these presents that I Tousen Kamecleur did claim on the 8 day of June one claim situated in the Spaulding district at the mouth of the French gulch known and designated as number one up and measureing one hundred feet up for mining purposes

I here by Certify that the above record was made on the 12 day of June 1860 at the request of Tousen Kamecleur in Person

Asher. A. Stevens
Secretary"

In spring, 1860, mining activity boomed in French Gulch. That summer, well over 1,000 men prospected and worked their claims.

Paige City

As early as spring, 1860, a miner's camp formed in French Gulch. *The Denver Evening Post* on July 17, 1897, noted the camps interesting history:

"...The first townsite was located on a sloping elevation overlooking the little channel from which the miners were shoveling the rich gravel into Long Toms, rockers and sluice boxes. The miners in those days confined their operations mainly to rim-rocks, bars and little draws, leaving the beds of the main channels virgin territory, up to the present time, with the exception of portions of Gold Run, the tributaries of the Swan and Nigger gulches. Water is an essential element for successful placer mining. It is also a serious obstacle. Being confined to the use of primitive facilities, the pioneer miners worked only such territory as could be handled by pick and shovel by men comparatively dry-shod. When one bar was worked down to the water level in the gulch, the miners would locate another and another, until they were leveled into immense beds of tailings lower down the stream.

The original camp was located by common consent on a spacious bar and side hill, supposed to be above the placer deposits. Here were clustered the miners' cabins around general supply stores, red plaint sideboards, faro counting rooms and Coryphee tents. While there were no edifices dedicated for divine worship, the big tent used for mass meetings on special occasions and as a dance hall at night, was placed at the disposal of any preacher who chanced to be in the gulch on the Sabbath. There were no church bells to call the faithful to worship on these occasions, but, like Rome, all trails led to the 'Big Tent' and Georgian, Missourian and down-easter stood together and listened to the word as it was explained by some earnest follower of the Master, who had perchance a good, paying claim in Illinois gulch or on Yuba Dam Bar, while his pulpit was in turn taken care of by the 'sky pilot' of Tamarack Nos. 2 or 3 above discovery.

History repeats itself, even in small places. The power of gold, though circumscribed by buckskin sacks, glass bottles and tin cans, caused the destruction of that flourishing little annex of Breckenridge as completely as the passing away of great cities in the past. Unlike their destruction, however, while not a stone was left unturned of the original site of Lincoln after it was accidentally discovered that the intra-mural territory was one vast deposit of auriferous gravel, the population did not disappear from the face of God's footstool. There was simply a change of base of the town from one side of the gulch to the other. The old camp was staked off into claims and the new townsite divided up into lots in a day. More logs were cut for cabins and the tents were transferred in time so that the night shifts and lookouts of the Kentucky palaces and Monte Carlos received their stipends in time to return them to the sources from whence they came ere the cocks crew on the ranches along the Big Muddy. Joy continued unconfined; the dance went on uninterrupted, save by the mandate of the caller requiring the ladies to be furnished with liquid refreshments.

The real estate men of old Lincoln estimate the value of their lots by the amount of gold nuggets and dust to the pan of gravel and dirt. They know that it was not safe to be considered the owners of very rich claims and by common consent they claimed that their properties were worth only a dollar to the pan—a valuation common in the district. Patriotism and yearnings for another glimpse of the gourd beside the spring, beneath the elm or butternut on the faraway farm, induced many to silently steal away in the night, their burros and cayuses laden to the ears with blankets and camping outfits covering golden treasures with which to lift mortgages and send their sons to feather cars in college prize (?). Others came, who in turn, paid for their bacon and drinks with dust weighed on scales regulated in reverse of the customs prevailing in more civilized and Christian communities. The digging of a cellar for winter storage of provisions led to the discovery that Lincoln No. 2 was on ground as rich in gold as the old town. It in turn went down the gulch, covering deeper the bedrock known to be lined with fortunes for those who will venture to strip the surface . . .

CHILE COLORADO."

The men originally named the town Paige (sometimes incorrectly spelled Page) City, recognizing the contributions of Greenleaf Paige. A post office, with Greenleaf's son, Prince W. Paige, as postmaster, opened in June, 1860. On August 1, 1861, the name changed from Paige City to Lincoln City, honoring Abraham Lincoln. Oliver P. Higgins assumed the duties of postmaster.

Never platted, the town grew rather rapidly. Twitty, in his December, 2010, *Lincoln Townsite* report for the U.S. Forest Service, wrote: "Paige City quickly took shape as an independent community because of its strategic location provided opportunity for entrepreneurs. The camp received traffic crossing over French Pass from South Park, it was a center to productive placers, and had a substantial population of miners. Breckenridge and Parkville were the nearest commercial centers, but were too far from middle French Gulch to satisfy the demand for goods and services. Given this, it is highly likely that entrepreneurs opened the camp's first businesses during 1860. Based on the evolution of similar mining camps, Paige City's initial businesses were probably a mercantile [general store], saloon, and restaurant."

Mining Claims in French Gulch

In August, 1860, Nat Weber and sons filed and worked a claim at the mouth of Weber Gulch, named for Nat. Fountain, exploring in upper Weber Gulch on August 15, 2000, discovered a still-in-place sluice box. (**Figure 5**) On return visits, he removed the boulders covering the upper part of the sluice. (**Figure 6**)

In 1872, Congress passed The General Mining Law, which required owners to survey and register their claims to keep them active. The government then issued a Mineral Survey number for each claim. In 1873, W.C. Ripley filed a claim in Weber Gulch and received Mineral Survey (MS) No. 65. By that time, Weber had deserted the claim and most had moved from the county. **Figure 7** shows a portion of that mineral survey along with Weber's bedrock flume.

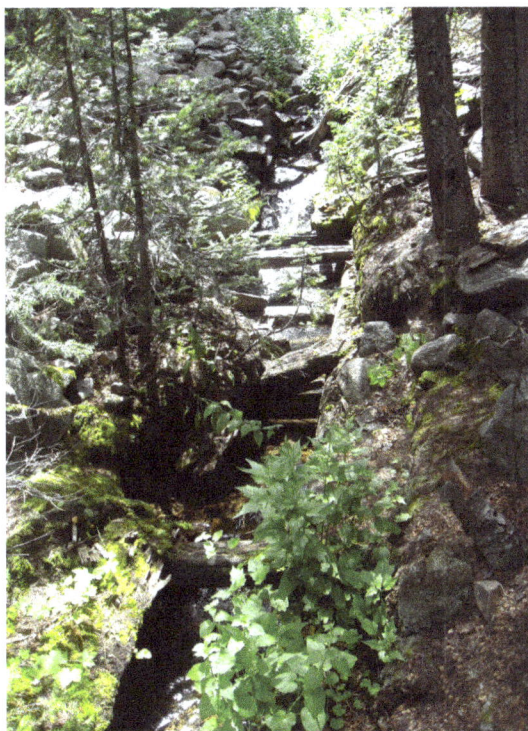

Figure 5. Nat Weber's Bedrock Flume in Upper Weber Gulch, 2000. Fountain discovered the flume on August 15, 2000. (Photograph by Author)

Figure 6. Nat Weber's Bedrock Flume after the Removal of Boulders. (Photograph by Author)

Figure 7. Nat Weber's Flume. (Photograph by Author)

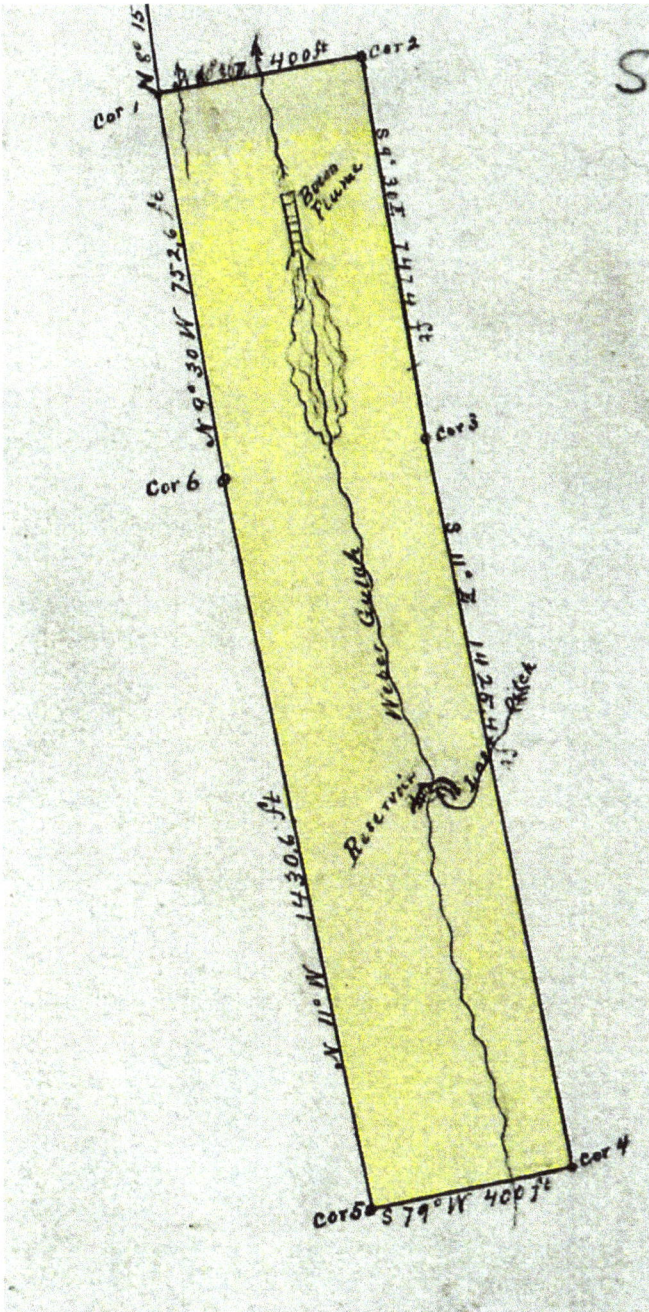

Figure 8. Portion of Mineral Survey (MS) No. 65, W.C. Ripley Placer Claim. Note the bedrock flume seen in Figures 5, 6, and 7. (Courtesy Bureau of Land Management)

On August 10, 1860, when Greenleaf Paige and sons, P.W., H.E., and T.A., worked their claim number 8, they netted a total of $400 (valued at $18 per ounce) for just their first half-day's efforts. During the summers of 1860 and 1861, they averaged $30 per man per day.

By September 20, 1860, the *Western Mountaineer* (Golden, Colorado) boasted that 150 miners in the gulch had reported at least $5 per day per man.

The *Rocky Mountain News* on October 8, 1860, added to the August 10 story:

"Mr. G. Page & Sons, have recently opened a claim near the head of French Gulch, and took out, in the first six hours run, with three hands, one hundred and four dollars and thirty cents; in that amount there were twenty nuggets which average two dollars and fifty-five cents each, and another one that weighed fourteen dollars and forty cents. The next day they took out with the same hands, eighty-nine dollars and ten cents, and are obtaining similar to the above every day. Mr. Cromey, who is washing close by Page & Sons, is taking out from ten to twenty-seven dollars per day to the hand, and many other claims are opening out finely.

It is thought by some, that the head of French Gulch, when fairly opened out, will prove as rich as the Georgia Gulch, from the fact that several promising quartz leads have been found to cross the head of it; among them are the Lincoln, the Webber and the Bruister leads. Dr. Adair, the recorder of the Lincoln lead, informs me that it is opened and yields forty-five cents to the pan of dirt, taken from the crevice, some fifteen feet from the surface, and that there is now a quartz mill on the road for that lead.

Mr. Richard Lacey, the discoverer of the Bruister lead, states that it is open, and prospects finely, so much so that Mr. Bruister is going to start East immediately, to bring out two mills, to be located on it. Mr. Lacey is an old California miner, and thinks the quartz out of the Bruister lead is very rich. Mr. N. Webber, the discoverer of the Webber lead, has now quite a pile of quartz already out, and one of Ellithrop's largest sized pulverizes on this claim. He is setting it up to run by water power, and designs having it in operation inside of ten days. He is very confident of having a rich thing; many other leads have been discovered, but not fairly tested yet . . .

W. A. S."

The November 7, 1860, *Rocky Mountain News* verified the excitement: ". . . We have had the pleasure of a call from Judge G. G. Bissell, of Breckinridge, who has favored us with some interesting information respecting the mines on the western slope of the Snowy Range . . .

French Gulch is about ten miles long; running into the Blue from the east, half a mile below Breckinridge. The streak is in some places difficult to find, in others very easy. In the best claims opened it is only about six feet to the Bed Rock. The stripping is about two feet, and remainder of the depth—four feet—is pay dirt. Claims that are open are paying from ten to twenty five dollars per day to the hand. Much coarse gold is found; nuggets of five to thirty dollars are common, and many of fifty to seventy dollars have been taken out, and one of over two pounds was reported, but the Judge doubts its authenticity. Many fortunes will doubtless be made in French Gulch the coming summer . . ."

Another New Mining District

In October, 1860, miners in French Gulch organized the Mineral Hill and West McNulty Mining District, located just west of Paige City. The Summit County Clerk and Recorder's Office holds the logbook for the new district but it does not appear on the 1880 map of all mining districts in the county. (**Figure 9** is a portion of that map.) Based on the location of the claims on Mineral Hill, the district most likely merged with the Bevin Mining District, which covered the same area.

Unfortunately, in transcribing the Mineral Hill and West McNulty logbook, another problem arose: legibility. Although the bylaws could not be read, Fountain counted 614 claims. Several miners held multiple claims.

Long after these original prospectors and miners abandoned their claims

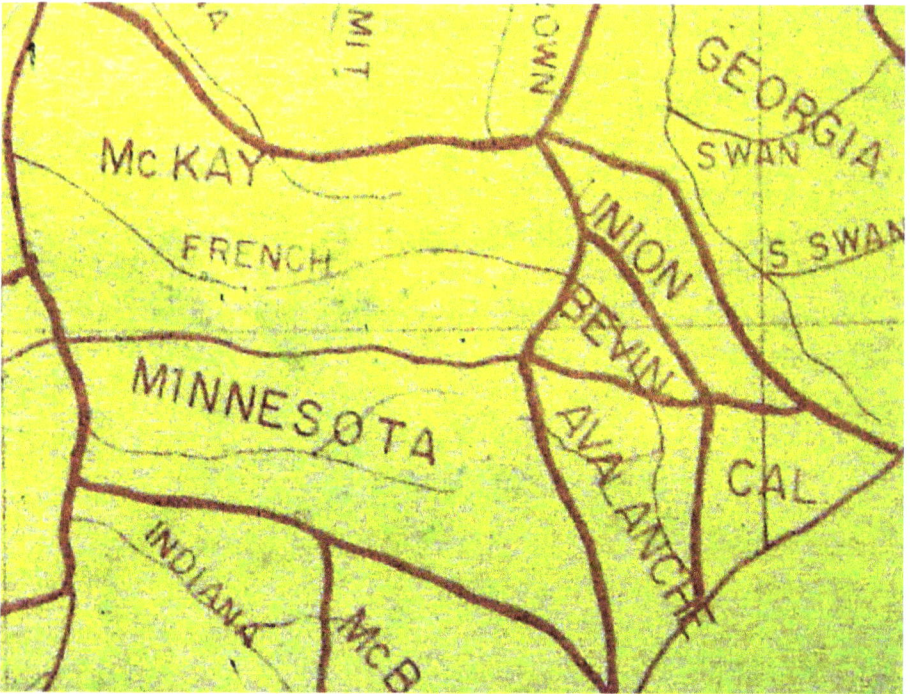

Figure 9. A Portion of an 1880 Map showing the Mining Districts in French Gulch. The map included the McKay, Bevin, and Avalanche mining districts. (Author's Collection)

on Mineral Hill, it became famous for rich lode claims such as the Cincinnati, Lucky, Minnie, and Rose of Breckenridge, among others.

Authors' Note: Lost logbooks and illegibility unfortunately are not rare. The Bevin and Avalanche Mining District logbooks have been lost. The McKay Mining District logbook is among those preserved in the county courthouse in Breckenridge.

McKay Mining District

The McKay Mining District, organized on February 26, 1861, included Gibson Gulch. The men elected George McKay, the organizer, president and appointed Pete Lacy secretary and recorder. The district bylaws followed a standard outline and appear here as written.

"Art 1#

It Shall be the Duty of the President & recorder to preside at all Meetings regarley Called & the recrder Shall Keep A correct Account of the Same & Keep the Books open for inspection at any time

Art 2#

The President Shall have the power of Calling A Meeting When he Sees proper or when 3 or more Miners Shall request him to call (?) he will Do it & he Shall preside over all trials & his Desion Shall be final & his fee Shall be $Two Dollars for each trial

Art 3#

It Shall be the Duty of the recorder to record all the Claims in the gulch & that he receives one dollar for each Certificate & that he preside at all Meetings & keep A correct Account of the Same & he Shall be paid for all trials that he presides at & his fee Shall be 2.50 for each trials

Art 4#

All Claims Shall extend 100 feet up & Down the gulch & 100 feet on each Side of the Center on the gulch & that each Claim ownr be Compeld to record those Claims

Art 5#

And if A Claim owner be Sick or Not Able to work his Claim he Shall Give So Notice of the Same & Know Claim Shall hold good unless Work Continud only By A Bonified Company and if that Co be working one of the Claims all the rest Shall hold good and all puretied[purchased?] Claims Shall be Worked under the Same said as preempted Claims

Art 6#

That know person Shall have A vote on this gulch but those that have A Certificae from the Recorder of the Gibson gulch under this persons organizasion & that all Aplescants coming

To Claim any intrest they Shall Apply to the Pesidnet of the gulch & hear thare Cose & if he sees proper he can call A Meeting of the Miners in the gulch & then give them A hearing & if the Miners of the gulch gives A two thirds vote for them to hold any intrest or not that the said shall be law

Art 7#

This Constituion & By Laws May be alterd or Amended By A two third vote of the Miners on the Gibson gulch

A Meeting Was Called on the 28th of feb 1861 to Adopt this Constitution & By Laws to govern the Miners of Gibson gulch W. B Sanders Moved to Adopt & it Was Carried & the Constitution & By laws Was Adopted"

On April 10, 1861, the men chose H.E.L. Myer to replace Lacy as secretary and recorder. At the next meeting, at 6:00 p.m. on May 25, 1861, the group passed numerous resolutions:

"1st. On motion of R. B. Chisholm & said motion being seconded by Jos. Carroll it was resolved that we should elect a new president & declare George McKay out of that office for non-attendance at meetings in this Dist.

2d. On motion of Jos. Carroll & said motion being seconded by Niel Sutherland Mr Long was duly elected to fulfill the vacant office for president of this District.

3d. Resolved: That every claim on this Gulch should be 100 feet up & down the Gulch & that the claim should be measured over correctly

4th. That this meeting should appoint two disinterested men who shall measure & stake off the claims to morrow & that where & on motion of L. L. Higby & seconded by L. L. Steele R. B. Chisholm & J. Belsom were appointed for this office

5th. On motion of R. B. Chisholm & seconded by L. L. Higby That every claim holder shall have the right to run his sluice boxes 50 feet or less down on the Claim below Rim & also to leave the tailings on the Claim below him."

By June, 1861, insufficient water in Gibson gulch prevented the men from working their claims. They decided on June 25 that "the claims of said Gulch should hold good without work or labor until there was water sufficient to work them." The next day, 15 miners representing 103 claims and E. Evenson signed an agreement "that would bring forty inches of water within a reasonable length of time to Gibson Gulch for the sum of two thousand dollars."

The McKay logbook included several sales during the summer of 1861:
May 24: Ed Paff, Peter Muhlebach, and Andrew Cantzler sold claim No. 5 above discovery claim to Thomas Thompson & Co. for $75.

June 8: Niel Sutherland sold claim No. 7 above discovery claim to H.E.L. Myer for $100.

June 8: R.B. Chisholm sold claim No. 2 above discovery claim to H.E.L. Myer for $500.

June 8: A. Cantzler & Peter Muhlbach sold claim Nos. 3 & 4 above discover claim to John Bolsom for $300.

June 12: Edner Myer sold claim Nos. 7 & 8 above discovery claim to E. Evers for $250.

July 2: A.G.H. Clinton & Co. sold claim Nos. 4 & 5 below discovery claim to Nettleton & Mason for $300.

July 2: Joseph Carroll & Co. sold claim No. 10 above discovery claim to S.B. Beedle & Co. for $150.

July 19: John L. Whiting & John J. Tompkin sold claim No. 1 above discovery claim to G.W. Pettleton, A.H.G. Clinton, & Thomas Mason for $300.

The last page of the McKay logbook contained some interesting information. From May, 1861, through January, 1862, the recorder wrote the day of the week on which each month started. A check of an 1861 calendar proved them correct. The recorder's name appeared but could not be read. Below that appeared the ominous notation:

Fort Sumter
South Carolina

. . . where troops fired the opening shots of the Civil War on April 12, 1861.

1861

Claim jumping occurred often throughout the mining areas of the county—even in French Gulch according to the *Rocky Mountain News* on January 21, 1861. Claim jumpers took advantage of those who left in the winter when it became too difficult to work a claim. Mining district bylaws always specified the number of months a claim owner must work the claim (generally June through September) and the months of guaranteed ownership if no work had been done on the claim. Surprisingly, about 150 men still worked their claims during January, despite snow depths of three to four feet in the gulch and six to eight feet on the mountains.

Population in French Gulch and Paige City increased. In a letter to the editor of the *Rocky Mountain News* dated May 11, 1861, the correspondent noted that where there had been few cabins the previous fall, the area for "miles around was now thickly set with rising habitations." He added that several hundred miners formed the Bald Mountain [Mining] District and voted to "require claims to be worked no later than June 15th."

In the latter part of May, miners who found a gold nugget weighing almost one full pound and valued at $283.50 declared it to be the largest nugget yet found in Summit County.

For years, the Fourth of July celebrations in Summit County outdid those for any other holiday in the year. The celebration in French Gulch provided a full day of activity according to the *Tarryall Weekly Miners Record*: "The anniversary of our Nation's Independence was celebrated for the first time in this [French] gulch, with much ceremony. The dawn was greeted with the discharge of volleys of small arms. Several flags were thrown in the breeze; there was an evening bonfire. A mass meeting was held at which Dr. Paige read a patriotic address. There were hearty cheers for the American Union and for Jeff Davis and the Confederacy. The citizens were reported to have been orderly, with little drunkenness." (July 13, 1861)

The *Tarryall Miners Record* confirmed the good reports on July 13, 1861:

"Lincoln City,

July 6, 1861

Business in the Gulch is very good, and provision and goods of all kinds, plenty and cheap. Building is going on very rapidly and everything wears a lively appearance. W. S. Waker & Company, have about completed a large two-story store, and will move in soon with their extensive stock of goods. Messrs. Barrett, Lyon & Company, have just erected a new house and filled it with a stock of goods—They do a large business and freight directly from the River here.

The Gulch is rapidly assuming an air of importance and will, in another season be 'the' Gulch of this side of the range."

By the summer of 1861, the population of Paige City increased daily. Merchants arrived. In July, Kastor & Co. of Denver established a clothing and furnishings store. The July 10, 1861, issue of *The Daily Colorado Republican and Rocky Mountain Herald* carried an advertisement for a "MEAT MARKET" in Lincoln City owned by G. Longton. The *Miners' Record* on July 20 announced that the town, "a respectable sized village with shops, hotels, and businesses houses," would henceforth be known as Lincoln City. Daniel Laughlin owned one of the hotels in Lincoln City, the Bella Union.

C.H. Blair remembered the Bella Union:

"The Memorable Ball at the Bella Union.

'I think the deep snow Christmas, the one when we had the ball at the Bella Union, beat anything that ever I saw,' said C. H. Blair, the old-timer, as he fingered his snowy beard.

'You've heard of the Bella Union, haven't you?

'What, the mine?

'No, the hotel—but of course you can't remember—that was before your time. The Bella Union was the main hotel at Lincoln, up near Breckenridge, and at the time I speak of, the Christmas of 1861, McLaughlin and Ford were running it, and I want to tell you there are plenty of hotels in these days that ain't half so good and mighty few that are better. It was big and roomy and those fellows knew how to get up good meals and they kept first-class whiskey and the house was popular.

'Well, on Christmas eve it was made up that we should have a big dance at the Bella Union the next night. The snow was four feet deep on the level and it was hard to get about, but we youngsters hustled and got the invites around and McLaughlin and Ford, assisted by a lot of volunteers, got everything ready for the blowout.

'A number of extra rooms were arranged for reception and a long hall was stopped up and the wind chinked out to make a supper hall. You see, they wanted the big dining room to dance in.

'Most of the women folks lived over in Georgia gulch. It was only two miles away, but the snow was so deep that getting the girls over was a problem. Finally after the boys had broken the road the best they could the women were piled into ox wagons and the procession started.

'Well, sir, you may not believe it, but it took just three hours to get them down to Lincoln. But they started early and it wasn't later than 9 when they all got there. Most of the women were miners' wives, but there was a fair sprinkling of young girls and you bet we all had the liveliest old time you ever read about.

The old pioneer laid the side of his head gently on his right palm and smiled, his eyes twinkling but looking nowhere, his mental vision gazing back at the gay scene of long ago in the dining room of the Bella Union.

'I can pretty nigh see her now,' he went on absently, 'a little pony-built girl—her name was Thompson—who seemed to me that night to be about the prettiest thing that ever slid over a floor. There were a few loose, puncheons that some of 'em tripped on, but when I and this little girl in green got to waltzing we never touched one of 'em. We flew—just flew, and we didn't seem ever to get tired. Ah-h-Ho,' sighed the old man, 'that was a great night!

'Old Bill Pollock—W. P. Pollock, now dead—played the fiddle; and say, he could just make a fellow dance, whether he felt like it or not. He played old-time tunes, and he put muscle into 'em and made 'em hum, you better believe. Most of us men had on our buckskin breeches stuffed in our boots. The women were diked up all right, though, and looked mighty nice.

'B. L. [Barney] Ford, one of the proprietors, was boss caterer and the supper was fine—just fine; and after that we danced again and kept it up all night. Lots of the women stayed all the next day, for the snow kept falling and it was still harder getting about.

'By George! do you know that thinking of this dance has helped my memory mightily? Now, for instance, I can call the names of a good many that enjoyed that fun. There was Hobe Murray, now living in Salida; Billy Reynolds and wife, now of Georgetown; O. B. Brown, who is at present a big manufacturer of woolen cloth back in Iowa; H. B. Haskell and wife and his pretty daughter Josie—she afterwards married a man by the name of Bassett, and he runs the Bassett saw mill down towards Palmer Lake.

'Then there was Bill Iliff, well known through the state, and Capt. Walker and wife, who now live in Silverton; and—oh, I could think up quite a number of others if I had a little time.

Again the pioneer paused and reflected, with a face that was sad, but still smiling. 'Yes, that was a great Christmas—a great dance. It wound up with a Virginia reel—a regular old hoe-down—and didn't we make those old boards talk!"

Father John Lewis Dyer

In March, 1862, Father John Lewis Dyer received a letter from Brother D.C. Dennis, presiding elder of the Rocky Mountain District, Kansas Conference, asking him to take charge of the Blue River Mission, Summit County, Colorado. He arrived in Parkville on April 2 and preached his first sermon there on Sunday, April 6, at 10:30 in the morning and then went to Lincoln City and preached in the afternoon. Dyer explains in his autobiography, *Snow-Shoe Itinerant*:

> "...I had a chance to buy a cabin in French Gulch or what was then called Lincoln City, and I set up in a humble way keeping bachelor's hall. My bedstead was made of pine poles, even to the springs. The bed was hay, with blankets for coverings. I slept well, and rested as well as though I had been in a fine parlor-chamber. My furniture was primitive and limited—a table, and a couple of boards against the side of the wall for a cupboard, six tin plates, half a set of knives and forks, with a few other indispensables; a coffee-pot, a tin cup, and a pot for boiling vegetables—when I had them—and a frying-pan. I had a few books to read—the Bible, hymn-book, and Methodist Discipline, with two of our weekly *Advocates* and *Rocky Mountain News*. I tried to keep up with the times ...

> We cooked by a fire-place, generally baking our bread in a frying-pan set up before the fire. I must not forget to say that we had stools and benches in place of chairs. There was one chair left in my house, made by some one out of crooked pine-limbs, with the seat of ropes. It was so comical that if I had it now, I would certainly place it in an exposition. It was easy enough for an editor.

> I tried to make my cabin useful. It was about eighteen feet square, and taken every way, the best place to hold our meetings. The floor

Figure 10. Father John Lewis Dyer. (Courtesy of the Summit Historical Society)

was hard ground. I got gunny-sacks and made carpet, and covered the table with two copies of the *Northwestern Christian Advocate*. And thus I preached to the people in my own house, not in a hired house, as the Apostle Paul did . . .

I will give an instance at Lincoln City, at our hotel. They must give a Christmas dinner, and, of course, a dance at night. I concluded to take dinner with them. The host made me no charge, as it would be what we old bachelors called a square meal. As I was about to leave, the ladies pleasantly invited me to stay to the dance. Of course I could not accept the invitation. But they said: 'You visit at our houses, and you ought to show us respect and stay.' At the last came the lady of the house, and said: 'this is an extra occasion, and it will be no harm for you to dance with me; why can't you, accept

Figure 11. Father Dyer and His Family. (Courtesy of the Summit Historical Society)

my offer?' The reply was: 'You're a lady, but not quite handsome enough for me to dance with.' She was taken back at that, and the others laughed, and I got out, as my cabin was only two hundred feet away. They soon fiddled me to sleep. But they danced till daylight, and often drank at the bar. Being full, and having no place to sleep, they went up to Walker's saloon. He made some hot sling, and that set them off. They declared that every man in town must get up, and the preacher should treat the company or make a temperance speech. It was just daylight when we heard them on the street, and as they had always passed me before, I turned the key and hoped they would do so again. But when they found the door fast they said: 'If you don't open it we will break it in.' I threw it open and invited them in; but they said: 'We have come to take you up to Walker's, and you either treat or make a temperance speech.' I requested them to let me eat breakfast first; but they said: 'You must go now.' I slipped out, leaving the door open, and went ahead of the company.

Soon there were over forty men, and they called a chairman or moderator; but they were too drunk to be moderated. I get upon a box and stated my arrest, and proposed to make the speech. They said: 'Go on.' I said: 'Gentlemen, first I will tell you what I think! There is not a man here but would be ashamed for his father, mother, sisters, or brothers, to know just our condition here this morning.' They stamped and roared out, 'That's so,' all over the house. 'And next,' I continued, 'if we were not so drunk, we would not be here' (Cheers, 'That's so, too!' all over the house.) I wound up and was about to take leave, but the judge said: 'I move that we vote that everything Mr. Dyer has said is true,' and they gave a rousing vote. He said, 'The ayes have it,' but that I must not go yet; and made and put a motion that they all give Mr. Dyer one dollar apiece; and that was also carried. They took the hat, got twenty dollars, and I thanked them and went home to breakfast …"

Lincoln City 1862

Lincoln City grew in 1862. The Summit County Board of County Commissioners met on April 21, 1862, with Patrick Smith, chairman, and Peter Muhlebach, commissioner, present. W.S. Walker and Daniel M. Laughlin presented their bonds and received their licenses, costing $50, to sell retail liquor in Lincoln City. The county clerk and recorder, Joseph Thatcher, entered a deed in the record book on April 12, 1862. W.H. Smith sold a log house with shake roof located on the north side of French Gulch that served as the "Express Office and residence of Perry Wiggins" to Gilbert Ecker for $40. In April, 1861, N. Bury and Richard W. Bury had built a house across the street from the Bella Union, a popular saloon and theatre. A year later, on April 16, 1862, Richard Bury filed a claim for a parcel not "exceeding 160 acres," which included the 100' by 40' lot and the house they had built on it.

In what might have been considered a ranch claim, it would have been located on the south side of the main street traversing Lincoln City. By that summer, Lincoln City had additional merchants. L.C. Miller opened a mercantile [general store] and miners' supply business. W.R. Pollack established Summit County's first school.

Langrishe & Dougherty's troup gave performances in Parkville and Delaware City as well as in Lincoln City. The *Rocky Mountain News* on July 22, 1862, explained that Langrishe & Dougherty's company had just returned to Parkville on April 11 after performing in Lincoln City.

Stilson Patch Mining District

On June 14, 1862, French Gulch miners organized the Stilson Patch Mining District (known as the Old Patch Diggings) with H. Stilson, president, and Marshal Silverthorn, recorder. A committee consisting of G.G. Bisslee, A.L. Smith, and J.C. Weeks drafted a set of bylaws and a constitution for the district. The miners met on July 13, 1862, at 10:00 a.m. to adopt the bylaws:

"1st Resolved The name of District Shall be Stilsons Patch.

2nd Resolved the boundries of the District Shall be on the North French Gulch on the East Utah or Nigger Gulch Dist on the South Detroit Dist and on the West Spalding and Independent District that the boundy North shall be the bed of French Gulch

3rd Resolved That the officers of the Dist shall consist of a President and Recorder whose term of Office shall continue one year.

4th Resolved That at the request of any five claim holders the President shall call a meeting of the dist giving three days Notice

5th Resolved That the Recorder shall receive Sleaking(?) claims the sum of 75c for Recording 50c Sleaking(?) 25c

6th Resolved That the size of claims shall be 100 feet square

7th Resolved That each claim shall be represented by at least three full days labor each week after the 20th day of July 1862 Provided that a bonified company working on one claim shall represent all the claims of Said company

8th Resolved That any person or persons owning a claim in this District and working by the day in Said District shall be considered as representing their claim

9th Resolved That any claim not represented according to the above Laws Shall be free to be taken by any person who will work the same immediately

10th Resolved That the annual meeting of the Miners of this District shall be should on the first day of July each succeeding year"

The rest of the logbook contained information about the claims, their owners, and sales.

Because the 1880 map of mining districts did not include the Stilson Patch Mining District (**Figure 9**), it most likely merged with the McKay Mining District, which included the area once part of the Stilson Patch Mining District.

A Visit to Lincoln City

On August 22, 1862, Hans Jacobes wrote a letter published in the September 4 *Weekly Commonwealth* about his visit to Lincoln City:

"... Upon arriving in a strange place, more particularly when one is tired, the uppermost thought in concerning a place to stop. Following this idea, assisted by instructions received from friends in Delaware, I arrived at the 'Planters' Inn,' kept by Mr. J. D. Clarke. The table is good for the mountains, the house neat, quiet and orderly, and that important item with weary travelers, the beds, as attractive as the cleanest of bedding and the freshest, cleanest hay can make them. Across the street is the 'Bella Union,' of which report speaks well.

There are, besides these hotels, two or three stores, bakeries, meat markets, a shoe shop and a saloon or two.

The miners are digging away in the gulch, and some are making big wages.—Mr. John Conners showed me a pile of dust taken out near here, containing between two and three hundred dollars, all of it coarse and wire gold, scarcely a particle of it would have gone through a common sieve.

Great excitement prevails among many here concerning a rich lode just discovered about a mile and a half from town. It has been christened the Calvin Lode, after Mr. Calvin Clarke, the discoverer.—The prospect hole is less than three feet deep, and a good crevice plainly visible for a width of about eight feet. The quartz looks as well as any I ever saw, and in very many pieces the gold is distinctly seen with the naked eye. I have specimens in my possession showing the gold thus . . ."

Jacobes mentioned the very rich Calvin lode, found about one and a half miles from Lincoln City. Clark and his family arrived in French Gulch in 1860. Clark's sister, Helen, married A.C. Albee on May 28, 1863, with Father John Dyer officiating. The Albee family had arrived in Lincoln City in 1862. Clark spent most of his life in French Gulch, owning many valuable claims.

New Postmasters

On September 15, 1862, Frederick Doepke became postmaster at the Lincoln City post office, only to be replaced two months later by Albert G. Townsend on December 23.

Wilson Mining District

In February, 1863, the miners in the Wilson Mining District indicated a desire to merge with the Spaulding Mining District. The Spaulding logbook followed the proceedings:

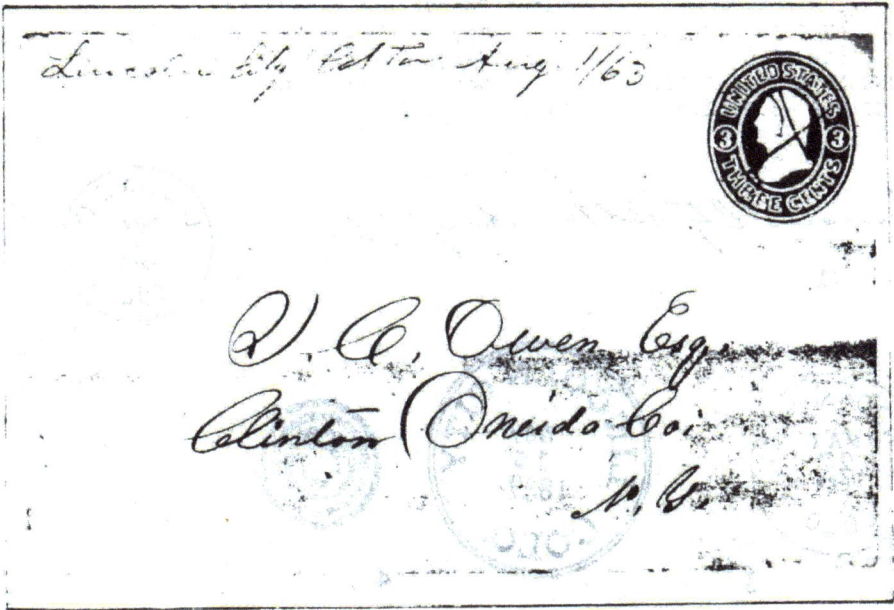

Figure 12. Post Card sent from Lincoln City, August 1, 1863. Prior to having or using a stamped cancel, postmasters and postmistresses used the "hand cancel" method seen here. (*Colorado Postal Historian*, Volume 16, Number 1, August, 2000)

"Breckinridge Feb 20 1863

At a called meeting of the minters of Spalding district the following resolution was presented and adopted

We the miners do attach that part of French Gulch known as Wilson district to Spalding mining district commencing at the junction of the Blue river & French gulch running up French gulch to Lincoln including French gulch to the East Bank   The following resolution was then presented and adopted that all claims taken up in French gulch should not be taken to obstruct miners of Union Patch from running tailing on said claims

E H Johnson
Secty"

"Claims in French gulch
Attached to the Spalding district

No 1 J W McIntyre
2 E R Williams
3 M Silverthorn
4 F C Kent
5 S J Mower
6 P M Haley
7 S Johnsen
8 G Muhlebach
9 P Muhlebach
10 J Muhlebach
11 G Kestenbader
12 F Bully
13 J N Brown
14 A Kincaid
15 E F Mowery
16 A Bolles
17 J A Madden
18 E H Johnson
19 D Fletcher
20 J A Pierce
21 G W Packer
22 H H McIntyre
23 M Kassal
24 This Kilak
25 F Pozanaski
26 W D McDonald
27 W Pozanaski
28 G W Rockafillozo
29 E Green
30 L G Tubbs
31 H Hannum
32 W Fleacher

33 Jas B Thorp
34 Wm Stilson
35 A Glick
36 R A Weeks"

Cemetery

Before towns established cemeteries, people buried their dead wherever seemed appropriate. On the left side of the road from French Gulch to Farncomb Hill, just east of Lincoln City, a wooden fence surrounds the lonely grave of William H. Milner. (**Figure 13**) The headstone bears this inscription:

"William H. Milner

Born
April 24, 1840

Died
May 8, 1864

Aged
24 years 14 d's

Dearest brother, thou hadst left us with thy loss
we deeply feel but it is God that has bereft us.
We can all our sorrows heal."

Historic newspapers in Colorado tell part of the story. Milner departed by coach from Blackhawk, Colorado, on March 25, 1864, with another passenger, W.C. Ripley, who held a claim in Weber Gulch. Ten days earlier, on March 15, an O. Milner, most likely William's brother, arrived by coach in Black Hawk. Two others with a last name of Milner appeared in the newspapers: July 25, 1865, Joseph Milner (*Rocky Mountain News*) and May 10, 1868, George Milner (*Daily Colorado Tribune*, Denver). Could these have been brothers of William?

On July 3, 2019, Fountain and Rich Skovlin visited the grave site and repaired the wooden fence. They removed vegetation and debris around Milner's grave looking for evidence of other graves. Their search proved successful; they found the rock outline of a double grave (**Figure 13**) and evidence of two other single graves but no wooden or stone grave markers. Could this have been Lincoln City's cemetery?

Figure 13. Grave Site of William H. Milner in French Gulch, east of Lincoln City, 2019. (Photograph by Author)

Figure 14. A Double Grave Site near that of William H. Milner, 2019. (Photograph by Author)

Lincoln City 1864

Many mining towns added "city" to their names to show prosperity and growth potential. Most eventually dropped the word. Although many maps used just Lincoln, newspapers for years referred to the town as Lincoln City.

Twitty explained:
"Lincoln saw its population and customer base decline until only a fraction remained by the end of 1864. The reason was that plenty of placer gold still remained in French Gulch, but it was too disbursed through the gravel to support the shovel-and-pan miners. The remaining placer deposits could pay if worked efficiently by company operations. Thus, regional interests formed partnerships, consoli-

dated groups of claims, purchased water rights, and invested capital in engineered infrastructure. Their success was due in large part to the above and the use of labor to process gravel in large quantities. When the individual miners went bust, they sold their claims to the company outfits and some even became employees. Thus, as hand-mining declined during the mid-1860s, the company operations rose in an inverse proportion. In 1863, investors organized the Flushing Flume Company to work the depleted gravel, and two years later, the Lincoln City Union Fluming company established an office in Lincoln. Three more companies went into business at Lincoln in 1867, including the Badger Gold Mining & Fluming Company, Grant Mining & Fluming Company, and Upper Fluming & Mining Company. Some of their miners lived in Lincoln, others lived at the workings but still patronized Lincoln's businesses, and the companies used the town as a center of commerce."

John and Catherine Sisler

In mid-year 1864, John Sisler (Sissler), age 45, arrived in the Breckenridge area to seek his fortune. He began his quest by filing 18 mining claims in French Gulch between July 5 and December 16, 1864. Two he filed jointly with S.J. Mower; the rest carried his name alone. Returning to Newry, Pennsylvania, that winter, he married Catherine (Katherine, Kate, Cate) Rhodes, age 22, on February 19, 1865. They left immediately for Breckenridge, Colorado Territory, arriving on June 29. A few years later, three of Sisler's claims in French Gulch, the Sisler placer, Ada placer, and Stillson patch, known as the Sisler properties, provided handsome rewards. (**Figure 15**) Sisler worked his claims with the help of hired men, including John Nolan.

John Sisler died at his residence, nicknamed The White House by locals, on November 8, 1883, at the age of 64. Catherine, who took over the management of the Sisler properties, quickly earned a reputation as an ambitious, savvy, and highly respected businesswoman. She invested in real estate, mining, and retailing—all while raising four children: Mary Anna, born July 3, 1867; Ada, born April 18, 1869; Charles (Charlie), born June 13, 1871; and Henrietta (Hattie), born June 17, 1873.

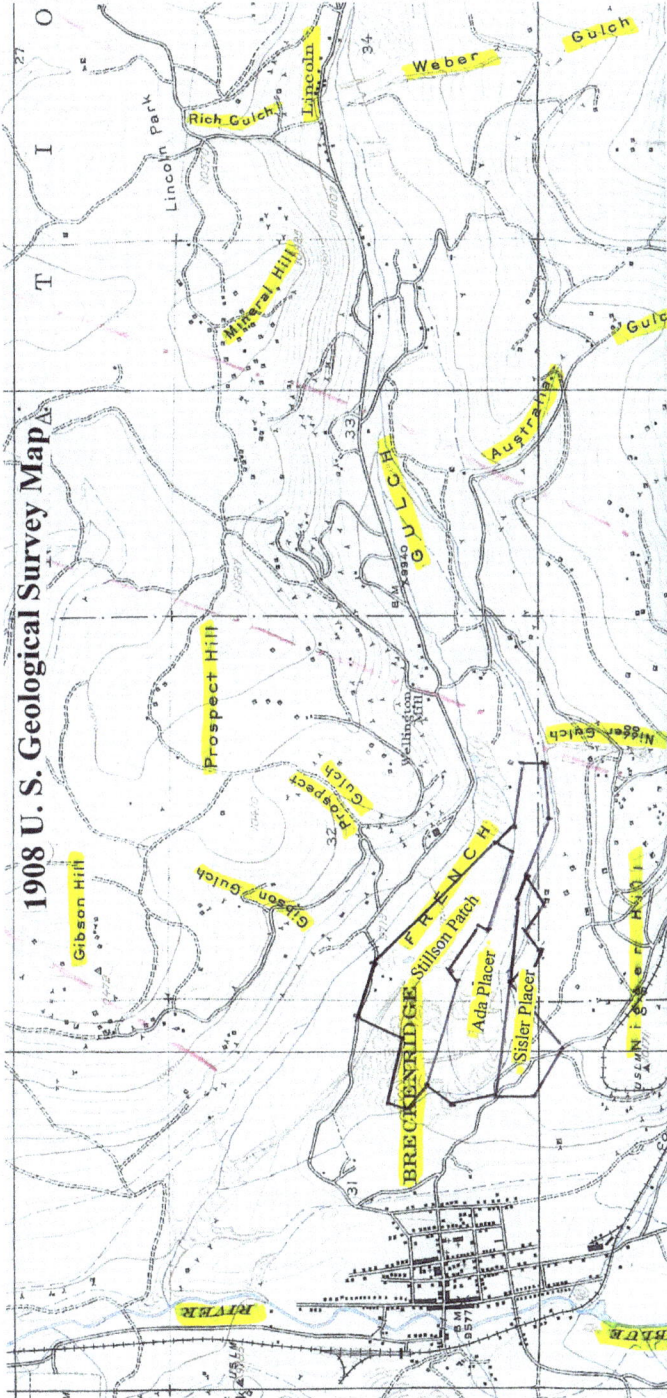

Figure 15. USGS Survey Map, 1908. The Sisler properties consisted of the Sisler placer, Ada placer, and Stillson patch, seen here near the mouth of French Gulch. (F.R. Ransome, USGS Professional Paper, No. 75)

Figure 16. The Sisler Placer, circa 1899. (Mary M. Marks photograph collection [cou-bha BHA.015]; From USU Special Collections, Merrill-Cazier Library. Courtesy Breckenridge History)

Figure 17. The Sisler Home known as the "White House" in French Gulch. (Mary M. Marks photograph collection [cou-bha BHA.015]; From USU Special Collections, Merrill-Cazier Library. Courtesy Breckenridge History)

Figure 18. Catherine Sisler Nolan, circa 1900. (Author's Collection)

On November 9, 1885, Catherine, now 42, married John Nolan, 47, the Irish placer miner who worked with the Sislers in French Gulch. Throughout his life, Nolan purchased claims in French Gulch as well as surrounding areas. On the day he died, September 21, 1888, he conveyed all his properties to his wife.

Catherine continued to manage the Sisler properties in French Gulch until 1900 when she sold them to the Mecca Gold Placer Mining Company. In 1904, a new company assumed ownership of the Sisler properties, renaming them the Mekka properties.

For detailed information about John and Catherine Sisler, read *Chasing the Dream, The Search for Gold in French Gulch, Breckenridge, Colorado,* by Fountain and Mather.

1868-1869

The gulch buzzed with activity as *The Rocky Mountain News* reported on July 17, 1868:

"...In French Gulch mining is carried on with great activity. Four different fluming companies are hard at work, and taking out good pay. McFadden & Maddon, Sisler and Mower, are working in Stilson Patch. Rippey [Ripley], Clark, Iliff and Todd are working in the gulch near Lincoln City. All hands are realizing large wages. Some new comers are about to lease Capt. [S.W.] Walker's stamp mill at Lincoln City to work ores from lodes near the city."

July 1, 1869, *The Colorado Miner* added:
"... In the gulch mining is moving briskly; hands are realizing from ten to twenty dollars each, per day. Mr. Calvin Clark, recently gathered from a bed-rock surface, of not more than 30 feet square, the net result of $1,500. Mr. Clark has discovered a new lode, which assays all the way from $75 to $1,300 per ton. The crevice is wide, and is mostly galena, mixed with copper pyrites, it is named the 'Tonkelson.' Mr. W. C. Rippy [Ripley] is endeavoring to open a belt of lodes that cross Weber Gulch, running through the Jeff Davis and Lillinadale patches, with a boom Ditch, the first one in that section."

The *Rocky Mountain News* on October 28, 1869, noted an African American among the miners:
"Doctor Bevan, member of the legislature from Summit county, is in town. Also W. C. Rippy [Ripley] of the same county. The remarkable discovery of silver ore by Negro Johnson, referred to in yesterday's *NEWS*, is said by them to be in or near Lincoln city, French gulch, Summit county, and that it is even richer than reported from Georgetown."

New Postmaster

The post office in Lincoln City welcomed Charles H. Blair as the new postmaster on March 10, 1870.

In July, 1871, the *Daily Register Call* (Central City) listed a blacksmith shop, post office, and a 60-stamp quartz mill run by water-power standing among many vacant buildings. The mill owned by W.S. Walker cost $13,000 but sat idle most of the year.

Figure 19. Lincoln City Post Office Cancel, May 27, 1869. (*Colorado Postal Historian*, Volume 16, Number 1, August, 2000)

But the *News* sounded an alarm—warning of the inevitable downturn with an economy based on a non-renewable resource:

"The rise of company operations in French Gulch should not be mistaken for long-term mining and a sound local economy. The on-going operations provided enough jobs and business patronage to support Lincoln, but this was destined to last only as long as the gold. When the companies began to exhaust their ground during the late 1860s, Lincoln entered another major transition period.

It remains unknown exactly when the above-named placer companies dissolved, but they and also lesser partnerships began suspending operations and discharging their miners even as new companies were arriving. The trend accelerated in 1870, the majority of workers moved on, and Lincoln's entrepreneurs closed their doors, leaving only the post office, a mercantile, and a black-smith shop as representative vestiges of a business district. Most of Lincoln's buildings were abandoned by 1871, and the town drew little interest for the subsequent four years."

The post office continued serving those in the area. On September 20, 1872, Mrs. May Day became postmistress. Her tenure lasted until June 20, 1873, when Charles Blair returned. Two months later, on September 5, a new postmaster, Henry Spears, took over.

Upper Weber Gulch

When in 1873, W.C. Ripley filed Mineral Survey (MS) No. 65 in upper Weber Gulch, other miners worked the area. In the summers of 2000, 2001, and 2002, Fountain hiked the upper gulch, documenting the remains. **Figure 20** is a compilation of several individual maps that Fountain used in his field research. Nat Weber's bedrock flume (**Figures 5, 6, 7,** and **9**) appears on the composite.

Uphill from the flume, Fountain found a dam that held water for the monitors mining the area hydraulically. To the east, a blacksmith shop still stands on a mine dump. Remnants of several log cabins and a boardinghouse with a cellar remain in fairly good condition. He located large dumps from lode mines nearby. Several water ditches tapped the water from Weber Creek.

Still higher on the hill, to the northeast, he found a log dam used for booming. In 1872, companies and individuals began using this economical form of placer mining to work low-grade deposits in the Breckenridge area. A wooden dam built at the head of a gulch created a reservoir for water. A self-activating gate opened when the reservoir filled, releasing the water. After the reservoir emptied, the gate closed automatically, allowing the reservoir to fill. The *Rocky Mountain News* credited W.C. Ripley with being one of the first to use a boom ditch. (October 28, 1869)

Fountain named this area with its numerous remnants of early mining activity "The Settlement."

Figure 20. Map showing Mining Claims in Upper Weber Gulch. Miners worked the area in the early 1860s and again in the 1870s and beyond. (Author's Collection)

Figure 21. Negro Gulch in 1890s. Renamed Ford Gulch, it bears the scars of booming that occurred almost 20 years earlier. (Courtesy Ed and Nancy Bathke)

Figure 22. Log Booming Dam in Upper Weber Gulch, 2009. W.C. Ripley built the dam in 1869. (Photograph by Author)

Figure 23. Rock and Earth Dam in Upper Weber Gulch, 2014. The dam stored water for hydraulic mining. Large monitors called "little giants" washed the gold-bearing gravel into the bedrock flume seen in Figures 5, 6, and 7. (Photograph by Author)

Figure 24. Blacksmith Shop on a Mine Dump in Upper Weber Gulch, 2009. (Photograph by Author)

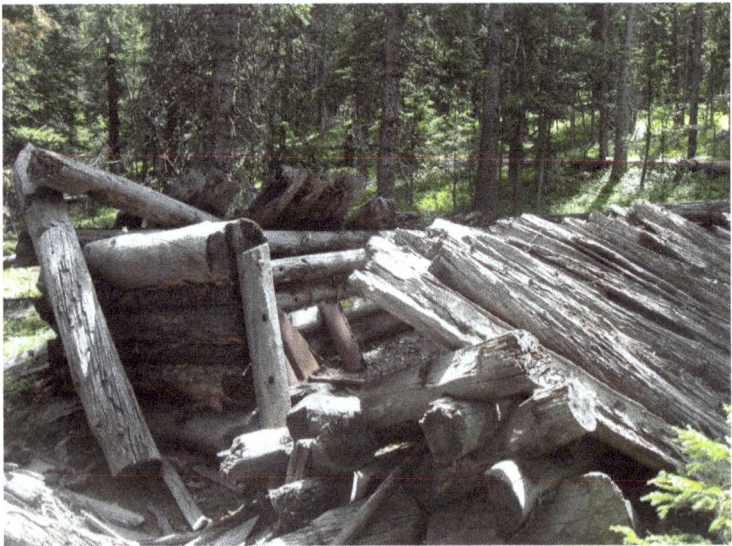

Figure 25. Miners' Cabin in Upper Weber Gulch, 2009. In this well-built cabin, dowels instead of nails held the door jam in place. The roof logs on the right interlocked, keeping out the rain. (Photograph by Author)

Figure 26. Windless Shaft in Upper Weber Gulch, 2019. Archivist Kris Ann Knish investigates the windless and cribbed shaft. The hand crank raised and lowered the ore bucket. (Photograph by Author)

Lincoln City Smelter

Twitty explained the need:

"The Cincinnati was among the handful of ore veins that prospectors discovered during the mid-1860s, and it was west of Lincoln and on the gulch's north wall. The prospectors found the ore to be a compound of gold, silver, and lead, and although they produced a small tonnage, they gave up within a short time because its complexity interfered with milling. The Cincinnati interests realized that a smelter was needed to treat the ore, but the necessary capital and engineering were beyond them.

A partnership known as Speer & Conant had the resources and knowledge for solving the problem presented by the Cincinnati's ore. In particular, they gathered the capital to buy the Cincinnati and build a smelter based on designs known to treat lead ores. At the same time, G.K. Gooding also wanted to build a smelter because he was aware of similar ore veins whose owners would develop them were a smelter available. To build a smelter, though, Gooding needed a reliable source of ore to keep his facility running in the meanwhile. In 1873, the two parties joined efforts as the Lincoln City Smelting Company and erected the Lincoln City Lead Works at Lincoln. Speer & Conant guaranteed enough Cincinnati ore to pay the smelter's operating costs while the other mines began production.

The residents in Lincoln placed great optimism in the combination mine and smelting operation. If successful, both had the potential to revive the town, restore a population, and bring entrepreneurs back. The smelter was key because it would be the only local ore treatment facility once finished. A wave of mine development was likely to follow as the smelter rendered previously uneconomical grades of ore profitable to produce. In addition, the smelter was supposed to support the Cincinnati, which Speer & Conant prepared for production. This mine was already reviving interest in the area's other mineralized veins. The Lincoln City company finally began treating ore in 1874, and although the smelter was a cooperative success, it proved a technical failure because the ore was not soft enough for the lead furnaces. Instead of abandoning the effort, however, the company refitted the furnaces. The town residents remained positive about the future and welcomed the present construction workers, who were the first newcomers since the gold rush.

By the fall of 1874, the company started the smelter again, and this time the operation was a success. Speer & Conant brought the Cincinnati into production, but the expected boom did not materialize because the smelter was only able to treat a narrow range of ore types, leaving most claim owners without the local market they hoped for. The smelter crew, some of the Cincinnati miners, and teamsters lived in Lincoln, but the total number was insufficient to support many businesses other than a mercantile and saloon ... Gooding and Speer & Conant sued each other over problems with the Lincoln City company, the smelter closed, and the workers were laid off."

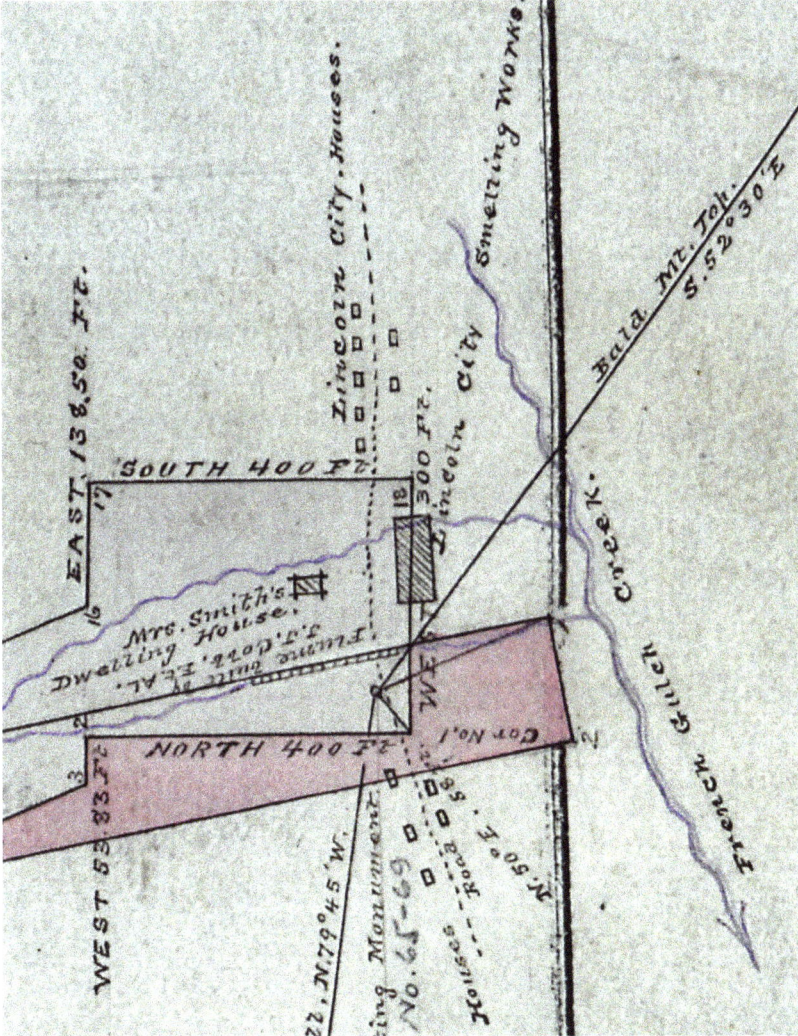

Figure 27. A Portion of Mineral Survey (MS) No. 187, August 1, 1875. This claim, owned by Mrs. Philena R. Smith and located in Rich Gulch, included part of Lincoln City. The illustration shows Mrs. Smith's residence, the road running through Lincoln City, several cabins, and the Lincoln City Smelting Works. (Courtesy Bureau of Land Management) [

Activity in 1878-1879

On March 12, 1878, Jasper K. Gooding assumed the role of postmaster in Lincoln City just as economic activity surged.

Twitty followed the renaissance:

"By 1878, local interests, primarily with Denver money, broke ground on claims around Lincoln including the Helen, Minnie, and Nebraska, and increased work at the Wire Patch, Elephant, and Ontario. Gooding saw this as an opportunity to revive the smelter, so he established the Lincoln City Silver Company, bought the smelter, and reopened the Cincinnati. The hardrock mines were not the only operations caught up in the boom. Local interests used the easy capital to rebuild an infrastructure for several company placers.

Figure 28. Road through Lincoln City. (*The Engineering and Mining Journal*, November 10, 1879)

The activity, road traffic, new mining offices, and the demand for goods and services awoke Lincoln from its dormancy. Archival sources are unclear about how many entrepreneurs opened businesses, and whether new buildings went up or the old ones remained, but the sources confirm that a population of 100 residents moved into the town."

The enlarged Gooding Smelter began operating again in the summer of 1879. It processed ores containing from $15 to $30 in silver and 60 percent lead from the Cincinnati, Shamrock, Champion, and other lodes.

Lincoln City War

Twitty explained the Lincoln City war:
"In 1878 or 1879, [Harry Farncomb] finally found the richest vein yet, and once this became common knowledge, other prospectors staked claims including the Little Morgan, Queen of the Forest, Triangle, Emperor, and Frederick the Great. Many if not all the claims featured gold veins that yielded almost as much as ground-surface, and mining capitalists quickly purchased some of the properties in entirety and others in part.

At this point, trouble began. Henry J. Litton, Patrick McCarty, Timothy Murphy, and L.B. Smart acquired the Ontario and American mines during or before 1882. All lived in Lincoln and operated several placer and hardrock mines, and ran the Lincoln City Quartz Mill to treat ore. When they discovered that the gold veins extended beyond the Ontario and American claims, and onto adjoining ground, they asserted that the extensions were theirs in entirety. Around the same time, James M. Strickler acquired a share in Farncomb's Elephant Mine, probably from Farncomb's partner Ebert. Strickler served in various government administrations in Denver since 1867 and was cashier of the Exchange Bank of Denver at the time.

Litton et al. immediately challenged Farncomb and Strickler both legally and physically. According to popular historical accounts, Litton et al. sued Farncomb and Strickler on grounds that Farncomb's original claims, which took in portions of the veins, applied to surface rights and not underground mineral rights. Of course, Farncomb and Strickler countered that their claims included mineral rights, and since Farncomb's claims were the first staked, they possessed discovery rights and therefore additional ground under common mining law. As the legal battles developed, both parties hastened to extract as much ore as possible in minimal time in case they lost the suit.

Several years passed with no resolution, and in impatience, Litton et al. dispatched gunmen to seize at least some of Farncomb's property. A battle ensued in which three were killed. Popular historical sources also claim that Strickler brought the Exchange Bank's weight to bear in the suit, ruining the bank. In 1885 or 1886, the court ordered the involved claims sold to a third party to resolve the dispute, and through manipulation, the Elephant and Ontario fell back into the hands of Strickler, Farncomb, Murphy, McCarty, and Litton, who formed uncomfortable partnerships to exchange their shares.

Although Lincoln residents tensed whenever these mine owners and gunmen were in town, the atmosphere was otherwise peaceful if not busy. The population was still 100 individuals in 1882, and archival sources note that it increased to 250 on a seasonal basis, reflecting a high proportion of temporary placer mine workers and prospectors. Popular literature claims that as many as 1,500 people lived in Lincoln at the time, but archival sources and material evidence in the townsite today do not support this figure. The number may have been true, however, for greater French Gulch."

1880s

The *Colorado Business Directory* of 1880 listed the population of Lincoln City as 100; businesses included the "Lincoln City Silver Co, gen'l store; Jefferson and Lincoln City Toll Road Co, J. K. Gooding, resident."

On February 9, 1880, Kleinschmidt & Eckhardt opened a steam-powered,

15-stamp mill in Lincoln City capable of reducing 15 tons of ore every 24 hours. The mill used wet crushing and amalgamated copper plates and blankets. The two-story frame building housing the mill measured 38 feet by 50 feet. The mill processed ores from the Elephant and Helm lodes. (*Leadville Weekly Herald*)

The *Herald* followed the growth of Lincoln City, which now had a smelter, stamp mill, store, post office, and a population of 150 souls, women and children included, that increased daily. The hard rock mines on Farncomb Hill produced some "big results." (March 14, 1880)

The *Herald* continued: Gooding and Ebert now partnered in operating the smelter and leading the company renamed the Lincoln City Silver Company. With a capacity of 10 tons per 24 hours, the smelter operated with one Cupola, two Drummond furnaces, and a 35-horsepower steam engine. The Cincinnati mine on Mineral Hill, under lease to Gooding, provided most of the ore for the smelter.

On May 8, 1880, the *Herald* described Lincoln City:

"... For a number of years past the town has been deserted during the winter months; but last fall everything having changed somewhat for the better, the people were induced to stay and look to their interests, and during the entire winter the population was greater than it has been at the same season for years. On entering the town, one is struck with the flavor of ancient prosperity that pervades the scene. The few houses left by destructive hands and warring elements bear indications of their years in the weakening foundations and well smoked timbers. What was once a lengthy street, lined with large mercantile houses, is now condensed into a country road, where a one-story grocery store that is saved from being solitary by a few bachelors' quarters and a miner's boarding house, is all that enforces the claim of town. The bed of the creek is denuded to bed-rock by the placer mining, and on the north slope of 'old Baldy,' the famous Jeff Davis Patch is cut up by giants into innumerable gulches, their intersecting banks rising into all manner of fantastic shapes and images ..."

The U.S. census taken June 22, 1880, showed the preponderance of miners living in Lincoln City:

Name	Age	Relation to Head of Household	Married or Single	Occupation
Eckhardt, Otto	37	Head	M	Lode Miner
Jennie	28	Wife	M	Keeping House
Faeg(?	22	Brother	S	Lode Miner
E. F.	4	Son	S	At Home
A. D.	2	Son	S	At Home
McMillan, Sallie	25	Boarder	S	Dress Maker
Thomas, Wm	45	Head	M	Lode Miner
Fraser, Robert	25	Partner	S	Lode Miner
Wilson, John R.	37	Head	S	Lode Miner
Hall, Wm. H.	35	Partner	S	Lode Miner
Schmidt, F. H.	27	Head	S	Lode Miner
A. W.	25	Brother	S	Lode Miner
Foote, R. W.	21	Partner	S	Laborer
Boland, Mich	35	Head	S	Laborer
Murphy, Timothy	46	Head	S	Lode Miner
Litten, A. G.	22	Partner	S	Lode Miner
Queen, Samuel	35	Partner	S	Lode Miner
Burt, James	21	Head	S	Blacksmith
Meeker, E. B.	35	Head	M	Lode Miner
E. F.	34	Wife	M	Keeping House
Edna L.	9	Daughter	S	At Home
Cora E.	7	Daughter	S	At Home
Walter E.	5	Son	S	At Home
Mary E.	5	Daughter	S	At Home
Card, James	56	Head	M	Lawyer
Lizzie	44	Wife	M	Keeping House
Morlin, Bevin	20	Boarder	S	Laborer
Moon, W. W.	25	Boarder	S	Laborer
Walsh, R. W.	34	Boarder	S	Laborer

Graves, John B.	45	Head	M	Laborer
Fannie	25	Wife	M	Keeping House
Fannie	4	Daughter	S	At Home
Eva	12-Jul	Daughter	S	At Home
Gorden, W.	59	Head	M	Carpenter
Emaly	37	Wife	M	Keeping House
Chas	26	Son	S	Laborer
Allen, James, W.	30	Head	M	Lode Miner
Kate	27	Wife	M	Keeping House
Allen R.	23	Brother	S	Lode Miner
Thompson, Thos	43	Boarder	S	Lode Miner
Caywood, Geo	23	Boarder	S	Lode Miner
McCarter, Wm	38	Boarder	S	Laborer
Silvey, Ross	19	Boarder	S	Laborer
Harvey, John	25	Head	S	Lode Miner
Jackson	20	Brother	S	Laborer
Davis, Thos	24	Partner	S	Laborer
Walsh, Alfred	29	Head	M	Laborer
Gertrude	22	Wife	M	Keeping House
Smith, Philena	55	Head	M	Keeping House
Blanchard, G. A.	47	Head	M	Carpenter
Luca	46	Wife	M	Keeping House
Eva M.	20	Daughter	S	(?) ocupa[tion]?
Allice D	9	Daughter	S	At Home
James A.	4	Son	S	At Home
Baker, John B.	52	Boarder	S	Lode Miner
Hunter, John	46	Boarder	M	Laborer
Clark, Geo M.	47	Head	S	Placer Miner
McMaunio, S. B.	34	Head	M	Keeping House
John F.	10	Son	S	At Home
Lillie	1	Daughter	S	At Home
Pulmeyer, A. F.	25	Head	S	Book Keeper
Jones, E. M.	38	Head	M	Laborer
W. H.	39	Partner	M	Teamster
Gooding, J. K.	46	Head	M	Smelting Works
S. E.	40	Wife	M	House Keeping

Chas	24	Son	S	Machinist
Clara S.	20	Daughter	S	Book Keeping
Jennie	14	Daughter	S	At Home
Hobkins, W. H.	21	Head	S	Laborer
Larrabee, A. I.	48	Head	S	Lode Miner
Clark, A. R.	29	Partner	S	Laborer
Perkins D. B.	45	Head	M	Lode Miner
A. E.	40	Wife	M	Keeping House
Geo B.	16	Son	S	Attending School
Phipps, K. C.	28	Boarder	M	Printer
Richard, Frank	23	Head	S	Butcher
Wheeler, D. B.	39	Head	M	Prop. Hotel
Elizeb. P.	35	Wife	M	Keeping House
Church, Henn	35	Cook	M	Cook in Hotel
Smith, Ford	49	Boarder	M	Lode Miner
Mischlin, Adone	27	Boarder	S	Lode Miner
Wall, A. K.	26	Boarder	S	Lode Miner
Hanly, John	23	Boarder	S	Lode Miner
Leatherman, C. W.	22	Boarder	S	Carpenter
Scybent, W. R.	26	Boarder	S	Laborer
Moore, S. W.	28	Boarder	S	Blacksmith
Anthony, D. H.	27	Boarder	S	Lode Miner
Adams, John C.	25	Head	S	Laborer
Z. B.	23	Brother	S	Laborer
Davis, S. C. B.	27	Partner	S	Laborer
Sankey, R. A.	40	Head	M	Attorney
Mary E.	33	Wife	M	Keeping House
Rodgers, John F.	40	Head	M	Traveler
Pennington, Maggie	25	Boarder	S	Dress Maker
Wildonen, John	30	Head	S	Lode Miner
Carol, Richard	35	Partner	M	Lode Miner
Farncomb, Harry	30	Head	S	Prop. Placer Mine
Geo	32	Brother	S	Supt. Placer Mine
Smith, Thomas	25	Employee	S	Placer Miner
Hain, H. C.	20	Employee	S	Placer Miner
Brown, G. H.	23	Employee	S	Cook

Hall, James	28	Head	S	Lode Miner
John B.	23	Brother	S	Placer Miner
McQueen, F.	21	Head	M	Placer Miner
Mary	16	Wife	M	Keeping House
Alex	7	Brother	S	At Home
Jackson, O. R.	23	Head	S	Lode Miner
Thing, Kent	30	Partner	S	Lode Miner
Westen, J. P.	32	Head	S	Lode Miner
J. N.	30	Brother	M	Lode Miner
Murphey, David	23	Partner	S	Lode Miner
Eudenifies, A.	20	Partner	S	Laborer
Hilderbrand, Jas	68	Head	S	Lode Miner
Kohnlsro(?)	28	Partner	S	Lode Miner

A total of 116 people lived in Lincoln City: 85 men, 16 women, and 15 children under the age of 18. The count included eight families, one attorney, two blacksmiths, two carpenters, two bookkeepers, two dressmakers, a hotel owner with several male boarders, a teamster, machinist, butcher, mine owner, and smelter owner in addition to the lode and placer miners.

R.W. (Robert) Foote, 21, lived in Lincoln City the first six months after arriving in Summit County. He would go on to be one of the wealthiest mine and business owners in the county, if not the state. Gooding and his family and Harry Farncomb, for whom Farncomb Hill was named, maintained homes in Lincoln City.

Crofutt's Grip-Sack Guide of Colorado in 1881 described Lincoln City:
"... is on French Gulch, four miles east from Breckenridge; population 150. One store, two hotels, the Wheeler and Perkins; three furnaces, one stamp mill—fifteen stamps—one steam saw mill, and several companies engaged in hydraulic mining, comprise the town."

On November 3, 1881, Alto E. Eckhardt became postmaster in Lincoln City. Towns established schools quickly. Sometimes the people funded the school themselves as happened in Lincoln City: "The people of Lincoln are awake in the matter of schools. Thursday night at a public meeting they raised one hundred and fifty dollars toward defraying the expenses of a five months term of school this winter." (*Summit County Journal*, November 29, 1884)

The Lincoln City school in 1881-82, part of Summit School District No. 5, served 18 students according to Mary Ellen Gilliland in her book, *Summit, 25th Anniversary Edition.*

The 1882 *Colorado Business Directory* for Lincoln City included:

"Mining town in Summit County, 4 miles east of Breckenridge. Tri-weekly mails. Population in the mining season, 250.

 Eckhardt & Co., mine contractors.

 Elyria Mining and Smelting Co., 15 stamp mill.

 Lincoln City Hotel, L. B. Wheeler, proprietor.

 Lincoln City Silver Co., gen'l mdse. And smelters.

 Lincoln City Stamp Mill, Geo. Meyers, supt."

In the summer of 1882, a road opened from the Ontario mine on Farncomb Hill to French Gulch just east of Lincoln for teams carrying ore from the Ontario mine to the Lincoln City stamp mill. County Road 567 follows the route today.

Figure 29. Road leading from the Ontario Mine on Farncomb Hill to just East of Lincoln, 1909. Teams used this road built in 1882 to carry ore from the Ontario mine to the Lincoln City stamp mill. (F.R. Ransome, USGS Professional Paper, No. 75)

Figure 30. The Ontario Mine on Farncomb Hill, 1890s. (Courtesy Ed and Nancy Bathke)

The 1883 *Colorado Business Directory* showed the growth of Lincoln City:
"Mining town in Summit County, 4 miles east of Breckenridge.
Tri-weekly mails. Population, during the mining season, 250.

> Breckenridge & Dubuque M. Co.
> Cunard M. Co. owners of Lucky mine.
> Colorado and New Mexico M. Co. operating the Rose of
> Breckenridge and oth'rs.
> Eckhart & Co. mine conts.
> Franklin Mine.
> Little Morgan Mine, Moore & Hunter.
> Lincoln City Hotel.
> Ontario Mine, Murphy, McCarty & Litton, owners."

The 1883 *Colorado Mining Directory* provided details about the mill:
"Lincoln City Quartz-mill in Lincoln; owners Timothy Murphy, Patrick
McCarty and Henry J. Litten, all Lincoln; building 30x50 feet, containing
fifteen Stamps, motive power supplied by a thirty-horse-power engine and

boiler; works erected on a patented five-acre mill site; capacity fifteen tons per day."

The *1884 Colorado Business Directory* showed more growth:

"Mining town in Summit County, 4 miles east of Breckenridge. Tri-weekly mails. Population, during the mining season, 250.

        Blanchard, Geo. A. carpenter.

        Card, James, teaming and express.

        Cincinnati Mine, Otto Eckhardt, leasee.

        Cunard M. Co. owners of Lucky mine.

        Colorado and New Mexico M. Co. operating the Rose of Breckenridge and oth'rs.

        Eckhart & Co. mine conts.

        Elephant Mine, Hayes, Murphy & Strickler.

        Franklin Mine.

        Little Morgan Mine, Moore & Hunter.

        Lincoln City Hotel.

        Ontario Mine, Murphy, Hayes & Strickler, owners."

On December 18, 1884, John D. Dayes became postmaster at Lincoln City. The 1885 *Colorado Business Directory* included even more entries:

"Mining town in Summit County, 4 miles east of Breckenridge. Tri-weekly mails. Population during the mining season, 250.

        Blanchard, Geo. A., carpenter.

        Boyes, J. D., postmaster.

        Cincinnati Mine, M. Musgrove, lessee.

        Cook, Cark, teamster, freighter.

        Colorado and New Mexico M. Co. operating the Rose of Breckenridge and oth'rs.

        Cunard M. Co. owners of Lucky mine.

        Eckhart & Co. mine conts.

        Eckhart House, Mrs. Ganger prop.

        Elephant Mine, Hayes, Murphy & Strickler.

        Franklin Mine.

        LeBounty, Jerome, teamster and freighter.

        Little Morgan Mine, Moore & Hunter.

Figure 31. Lincoln City as seen from Farncomb Hill, 1885. (*Crofutt's Grip-Sack Guide of Colorado*, 1885)

> Lincoln City Hotel, G. F. Williams, prop.
> Ontario Mine, Murphy, Hayes & Strickler, owners.
> Perkins, Geo. D., groceries and gen'l hardware.
> Shea & Cook, saloon."

Twitty provided greater detail:

> "Lincoln reached a peak around 1885. The proven mines continued to produce, prospectors were at work on other claims, and E.C. Moody, who found several important gold veins elsewhere, discovered yet another wire gold formation. Although the Lincoln City Silver Company and smelter collapsed under litigation again in 1882, the rest of the operations not only made up for the loss, but also justified several more mills in Lincoln. In 1885 and 1886, L.B. Wheeler and mine contractor George Blanchard erected small stamp mills, the Ryan & Hartman Mill treated ore from Farncomb Hill mines, the Walker Mill started up, and the owners of the

Lincoln City Stamp Mill sold to Frederick Smith. Several of the mills were on the edge of Lincoln, and the rest were nearby.

The number and diversity of new businesses, and especially lodging, paralleled the rise in milling. Further, some of the entrepreneurs were women, and others were also principals in local mining ventures. In 1885, G.F. Williams bought the Lincoln Hotel, and Otto Eckhardt and a Mrs. Granger opened the Eckhardt House. Eckhardt not only continued his contracting business, but also leased the Cincinnati Mine. George D. Perkins started the Perkins Hotel and a mercantile, and C. Shea managed the Shea & Cook Saloon. The high volume of freight traffic kept three teamsters busy, including James Card, Jerome LeBounty, and Cook & Clark. In 1886, G.P. Nelson stocked a second mercantile, and A.P. Williams opened a second saloon and hotel. Lincoln still had an in-town population of 250 and a sawmill producing needed lumber."

On April 9, 1886, George P. Nelson became postmaster in Lincoln City. The 1886 *Colorado Business Directory* - Lincoln City:
"Mining town in Summit County, 4 miles east of Breckenridge. Tri-weekly mails. Population during the mining season, 250.

        Blanchard, Geo. A., carpenter.
        Boyes, J. D., postmaster.
        Card, James, teaming.
        Lincoln City Hotel, G. F. Williams, prop.
        Nelson, G. P., Saloon.
        Perkins, Geo. D., groceries.
        Shea, C., saloon.
        Williams, A. G., saloon and hotel."

Lincoln City took their elections seriously. At the Tuesday, November 8, 1887, election in Precinct No. 8, G.A. Williams, E.H. Clark, and J.W. Helen served as Judges of Election; W. Osgood and Geo. D. Perkins filled the duties of Clerks of Election.

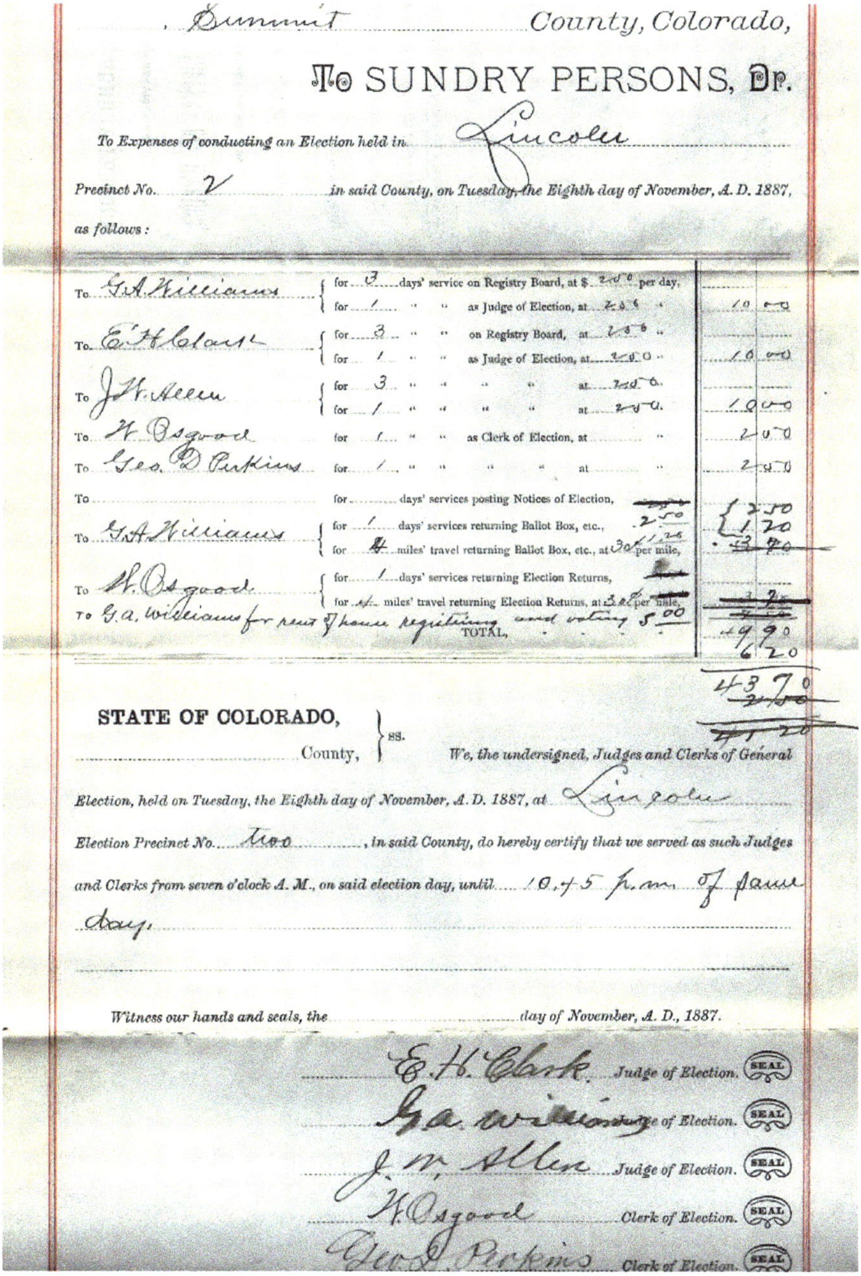

Summit County, Colorado,

To SUNDRY PERSONS, Dr.

To Expenses of conducting an Election held in Lincoln

Precinct No. 2 in said County, on Tuesday, the Eighth day of November, A. D. 1887, as follows:

To G.A. Williams	for 3 days' service on Registry Board, at $2.00 per day,	
	for 1 " " as Judge of Election, at 2.00 "	10.00
To E.H. Clark	for 3 " " on Registry Board, at 2.00 "	
	for 1 " " as Judge of Election, at 2.00 "	10.00
To J.M. Allen	for 3 " " " " at 2.00	
	for 1 " " " " at 2.00	10.00
To H. Osgood	for 1 " " as Clerk of Election, at "	2.00
To Geo. D. Perkins	for 1 " " " " at "	2.00
To	for ... days' services posting Notices of Election,	
To G.A. Williams	for 1 days' services returning Ballot Box, etc., 2.50	2.50
	for 4 miles' travel returning Ballot Box, etc., at 30¢ per mile, 1.20	1.20
To H. Osgood	for 1 days' services returning Election Returns,	
	for 4 miles' travel returning Election Returns, at 30¢ per mile,	
To G.a. Williams for rent of house registering and voting 5.00 TOTAL,		6.20
		43.70
		41.20

STATE OF COLORADO, County, } ss.

We, the undersigned, Judges and Clerks of General Election, held on Tuesday, the Eighth day of November, A. D. 1887, at Lincoln Election Precinct No. two, in said County, do hereby certify that we served as such Judges and Clerks from seven o'clock A. M., on said election day, until 10.45 p.m. of same day.

Witness our hands and seals, the ... day of November, A. D., 1887.

E.H. Clark. Judge of Election. (SEAL)

G.a. Williams Judge of Election. (SEAL)

J.M. Allen Judge of Election. (SEAL)

H. Osgood Clerk of Election. (SEAL)

Geo. D. Perkins Clerk of Election. (SEAL)

Figure 32. Expense Voucher with the names of the Lincoln City Judges of Election and Clerks of Election, 1887. G.A. Williams received $5 for "rent of house registering and voting." (Author's Collection)

1890s

Twitty recognized the downturn of the 1880s:

"Aware of the decline in mining, Western legislators passed the Sherman Silver Purchase Act in 1890 to reinstate Federal price supports for silver. The increased value restored confidence in silver properties and had the desired effect of stabilizing the overall industry. Whereas French Gulch may have otherwise continued to decline, its active mines maintained steady but limited production. Curiously, those that closed during the late 1880s due to low silver prices, such as the Cincinnati, remained idle despite the positive economic conditions. Lincoln's population hovered around 50, and the residents adjusted to the loss of customers and slower economy. W.G. Trapp bought the last solvent mercantile and George Blanchard focused on his sawmill. Although not mentioned in archival sources, it also seems likely that one hotel stayed in business and probably also served as a saloon and restaurant. The other hotels either closed or were converted into boardinghouses for local workers."

On January 23, 1890, Lincoln City welcomed its new postmaster, George A. Blanchard.

Twitty continued:

"At the end of 1893, anti-silver reformers in the Federal government repealed the Sherman Silver Purchase Act, causing the value of silver to fall to an all-time low. The mining industry collapsed throughout Colorado and across the west, and contributed to an economic depression that lasted through most of the 1890s. In French Gulch, the industry contracted around the Lucky, Minnie, and Wire Patch mines and even these operated at reduced levels. Lincoln suffered deeply and was nearly abandoned. The population fell to only 25 residents, the Postal Service revoked the post office in 1894, and it remains uncertain whether any businesses survived."

Figure 33. Laurium Postmark, June 9, 1896. (*Colorado Postal Historian*, Volume 16, Number 1, August, 2000)

Augusta Perkins served as postmistress from May 25 until July 10, 1894, when the postal service closed the office. The town's population, now numbering 25, traveled to Wapiti for their mail.

But as happened so often in other mining towns, the population of Lincoln City increased the following spring. The town once again warranted a post office. Postal regulations by this time would not allow a post office to reopen in a town using a former name. The new post office, named Laurium, opened May 6, 1895, with J. Roland Wilson as postmaster.

Speculation hints that the actual location of the Laurium post office might have been slightly east of Lincoln City, near the Milner gravesite (**Figure 13**), on the road leading to Farncomb Hill.

The Laurium post office should not be confused with or linked to the Laurium mine located in Illinois Gulch.

Lincoln City residents, part of Precinct No. 8, helped with voting in the Lincoln City schoolhouse.

On November 5, 1895, Judges of Election, John R. Wilson, Thos. D. Fisher, and Augusta E. Perkins; Clerks of Election, W.H. Strickler and M.S. McLeod.

On Tuesday, November 2, 1897, Judges of Election, Anna Williams, A.M. Rich, and J.A. Willoughby; Clerks of Election, Grant Kirts and Geo. E. Clark.

On Tuesday, November 8, 1898, Judges of Election, A.M. Rich, Sarah Burdett, and George E. Clark; Clerks of Election, Eli Burdett and M.S. McLeod.

On Tuesday, November 7, 1899, Judges of Election, Eli Burdett, Sarah Burdett, and A. M. Rich; Clerks of Election, M.S. McLeod and H.W. Smith.

Twitty expressed the optimism felt in Lincoln City:
"The wave began around 1899 when the core group of mines around Lincoln hired more workers, enlarged operations, and increased their output. Within two years, the movement in French Gulch became a revival as investors reopened long-idle mines, including previous producers such as the Cincinnati and Helen. The demand for lodging, meals, and basic provisions restored signs of life in Lincoln, and the population rebounded to 50. Ironically, the Postal Service cancelled the Laurium post office just as the revival was beginning and refused to reinstate it a second time."

The post office closed on April 1, 1899; residents now traveled to Breckenridge for their mail.

Early 1900s

On Tuesday, November 8, 1904, residents continued serving as election offi-cials for Precinct No. 8: Judges of Election, S.S. Woodberry, Eli Burdett, and M.S. McLeod; Clerks of Election, Paul Burdett and Omer Loeser.
Twitty used available evidence to interpret changing fortunes:
"Here, archival sources make no further mention of Lincoln, requiring us to interpret its history from industry trends in the area. As in previous years, Lincoln's in-town population represented a greater number of workers living at the surrounding mines. Six substantial operations in the immediate area employed dozens of workers, and smaller parties developed prospects and lesser producers. The Reliance Dredge processed gravel on the floor of

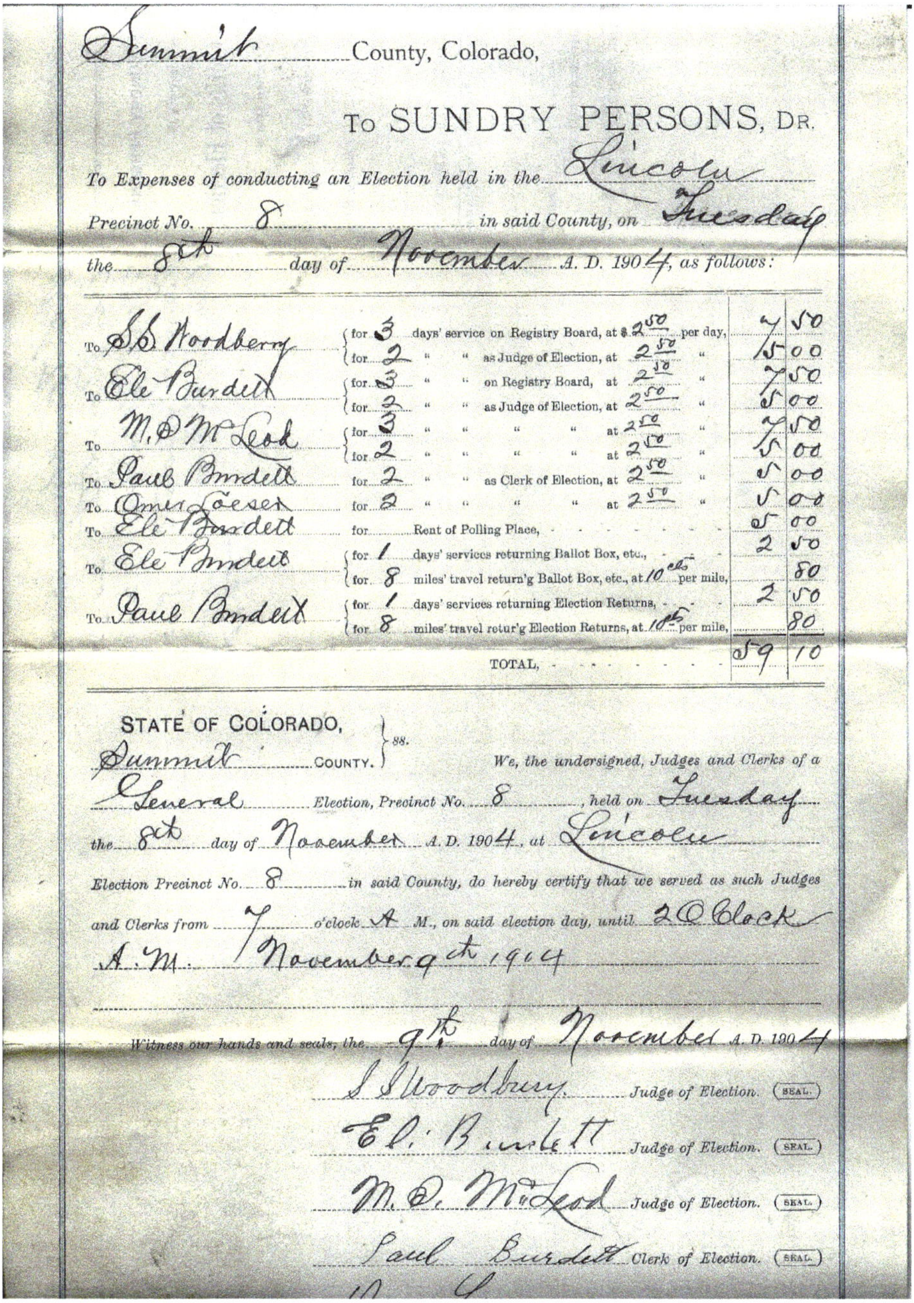

Summit County, Colorado,

To SUNDRY PERSONS, Dr.

To Expenses of conducting an Election held in the Lincoln

Precinct No. 8 *in said County, on* Tuesday

the 8th *day of* November *A. D. 190*4, *as follows:*

To S S Woodberry	for 3 days' service on Registry Board, at $2.50 per day,	7 50
	for 2 " " as Judge of Election, at 2.50 "	5 00
To Ele Burdett	for 3 " " on Registry Board, at 2.50 "	7 50
	for 2 " " as Judge of Election, at 2.50 "	5 00
To M. D. McLeod	for 3 " " " " at 2.50 "	7 50
	for 2 " " " " at 2.50 "	5 00
To Paul Burdett	for 2 " " as Clerk of Election, at 2.50 "	5 00
To Omer Loeser	for 2 " " " " at 2.50 "	5 00
To Ele Burdett	for Rent of Polling Place,	5 00
To Ele Burdett	for 1 days' services returning Ballot Box, etc.,	2 50
	for 8 miles' travel return'g Ballot Box, etc., at 10 cts per mile,	80
To Paul Burdett	for 1 days' services returning Election Returns,	2 50
	for 8 miles' travel retur'g Election Returns, at 10 cts per mile,	80
	TOTAL,	59 10

STATE OF COLORADO, Summit COUNTY. } ss.

We, the undersigned, Judges and Clerks of a General *Election, Precinct No.* 8, *held on* Tuesday *the* 8th *day of* November *A. D. 190*4, *at* Lincoln *Election Precinct No.* 8 *in said County, do hereby certify that we served as such Judges and Clerks from* 7 *o'clock* A *M., on said election day, until* 2 O Clock A. M. November 9th 1904

Witness our hands and seals, the 9th *day of* November *A. D. 190*4

S S Woodbury *Judge of Election.* (SEAL.)

El. Burdett *Judge of Election.* (SEAL.)

M. D. McLeod *Judge of Election.* (SEAL.)

Paul Burdett *Clerk of Election.* (SEAL.)

Figure 34. Expense Voucher showing Names of Lincoln City Judges of Election and Clerks of Election, 1904. (Author's Collection)

French Gulch, and several companies still sifted through tailings left from the gold rush. George Blanchard also continued to produce lumber, and he was probably not the only logging outfit near Lincoln. All these industrial operations and the population of French Gulch were almost certainly enough to support a basic set of businesses in Lincoln. The population and activity level of the early 1900s were similar in scale to the late 1870s, when Lincoln had a mercantile and combination hotel, dining room, and saloon. Several teamsters also operated out of Lincoln at the time. We can therefore assume that Lincoln had a similar set of businesses by the early 1900s. Instead of a hotel, however, boardinghouses provided most of the rented lodging, including the two opened by Mrs. C. Williams and Susan Wilson in 1898.

As with Lincoln's previous boom periods, an economic recession and declining metals prices forced all but the most efficient mines to close. In addition, the older workings were finally exhausted of rich ore, leaving low-grade material that was unprofitable to produce. The recession struck in the middle of 1907 and had its greatest impact the next year, leaving only the Lucky and Wire Patch mines, and Reliance Dredge in operation. Repeating what was now a well-worn pattern, workers left the area, the population fell, and Lincoln's businesses struggled to stay open. When the economy recovered by 1910, mining in French Gulch changed little and there was no revival. The same handful of mines continued to operate, but their employee base was too small to keep Lincoln's businesses alive. Thus, it can be assumed that when the mining industry contracted in 1908, Lincoln's last remaining businesses closed and most of the people left . . ."

The editor of the *Summit County Journal* had a sense of humor:
"On Thursday a lady visiting in town from the Pacific coast resolved to visit the 'city' of Lincoln, Summit county, of which she had heard her friends speak so oft. The stranger was led to believe that Lincoln was a town of at least 1,000 population. She accepted the

Figure 35. French Gulch and the Tenmile Range from Farncomb Hill. The cabin on the right sits on the Ontario claim. (F.R. Ransome, USGS Professional Paper, No. 75)

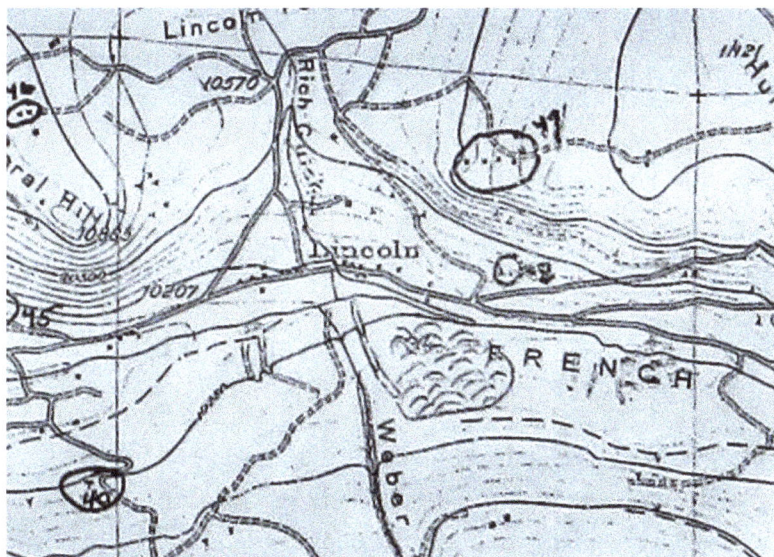

Figure 36. Portion of 1909 Map of Lincoln City. (F.R. Ransome, USGS Professional Paper, No. 75)

invitation of a friend to spend the day at one of the leading hotels there, where they were to take dinner, and in the afternoon enjoy a trolley ride to and from the famous mineral springs situate near the source of French gulch.

The trip was made; the visitor saw picturesque Lincoln and its surroundings, and she returned to Breckenridge—but the JOURNAL hasn't the courage to publish what she said." (October 11, 1902)

We wonder what the lady said?

Others visited Lincoln City: in August, 1916, Mr. and Mrs. Claude Colton of New York City visited F.E. Jacot, her brother; and on September 1, 1916, Mrs. F.E. Jacot and daughter returned to Denver after visiting for the summer. (**Figures 50, 54**)

Figure 37 shows Lincoln City in 1923. Twitty explained: "The north overview depicts Lincoln in 1923, after the town was mostly deserted. Rich Creek descends center from Lincoln Park down to French Gulch. The road crossing through the townsite is today's French Gulch Road. Where possible, the townsite's existing features have been labeled on the photo:

> F2: Garage;
> F3: Cabin;
> F11: House;
> F17: Blacksmith Shop;
> F18: Commercial Building;
> F19: Boardinghouse;
> F24: Residence;
> F26: Cabin;
> F28: Cabin;
> F36: Tunnel and Waster Rock.

Buildings no longer clearly represented in the townsite:

> A: a platform buried by debris;
> B: a platform destroyed by a recent driveway;
> C: probably a mill whose platform is totally overgrown;
> D: cabin whose platform is hidden by sod."

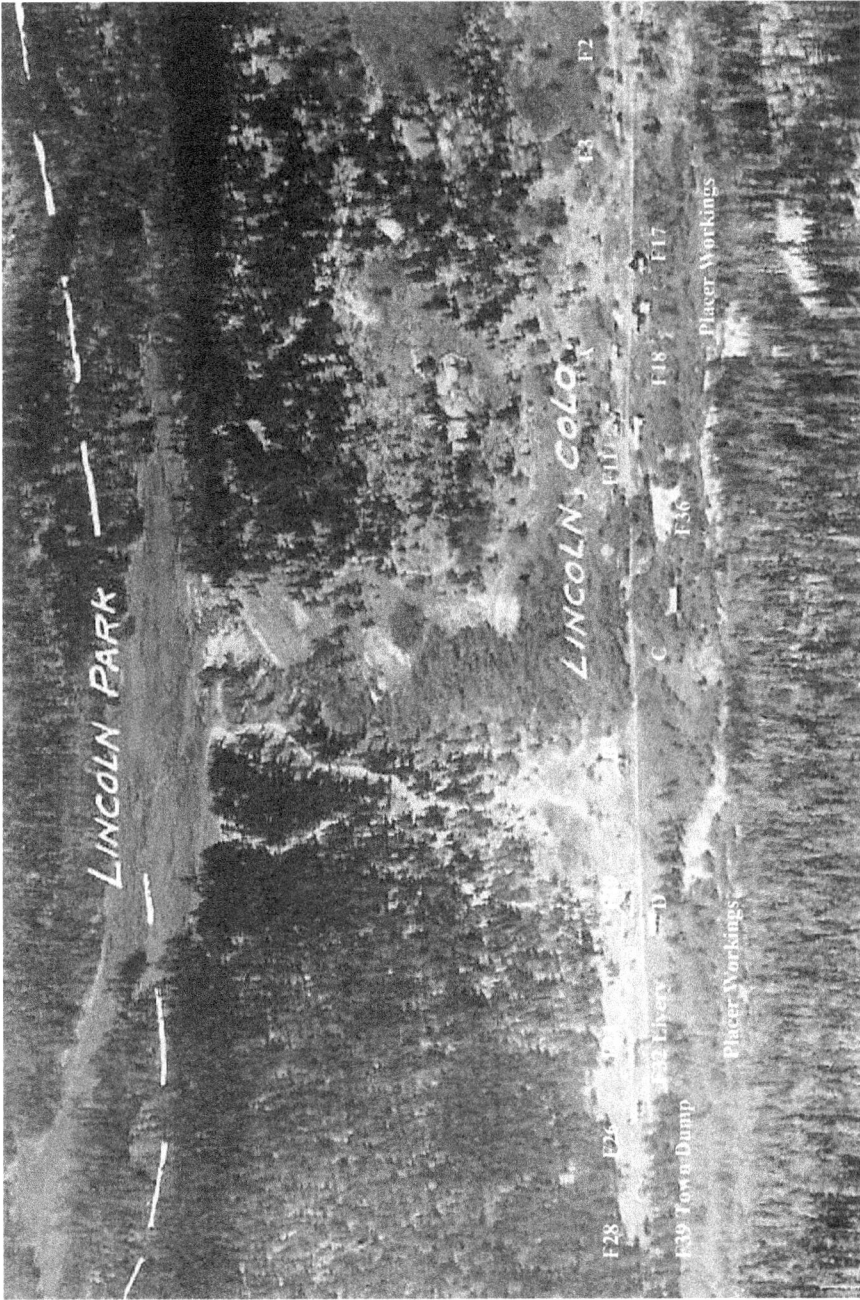

Figure 37. Lincoln City, 1923. By this time, only a few buildings remained. (Author's Collection)

Despite depressed markets for minerals, the *Herald Democrat* on March 4, 1924, learned that a new chain stamp mill with 15 stamps and a 35-horsepower motor began operating in Lincoln City on February 25.

The Turner Family

James Martin Turner and his wife, Louisa, lived in Alexis, Illinois. On March 2, 1882, she gave birth to their son, Harry Louis, three months before dying of typhoid fever. Turner made the decision to head west, leaving his son with his mother.

Arriving in Lincoln City in late 1882 or early 1883, he opened a sawmill. By 1887, his young son had joined him. Hoping for increased business serving a mine south of Breckenridge, he moved the sawmill to Hoosier Pass. When the mine failed, Turner faced financial ruin and lost the sawmill. Turner and his son moved to Cripple Creek, Colorado.

Harry, Turner's son, married Harriet Brace on June 3, 1906, in Victor, Colorado. Ten children were born between 1907 and 1925. The family moved often: Kansas in 1910; South Canon, Colorado, in 1920; Teller County in 1930; Glenwood Springs, Colorado, in 1940; Pueblo, Colorado, in 1950; and Silver Cliff, Colorado, in 1967.

Harry carried a small Kodak bellows camera with him wherever he went, hoping to document his surroundings. Even during the Depression and facing financial constraints, Harry explored small towns and rural areas of the west, often alone but sharing the experience with his family through hundreds of photographs. Miraculously, the family preserved the photographs through successive moves. Two of these photographs show Lincoln City, one in 1925 and 1942. (**Figures 38, 40**)

Approximately in 2005, Fountain and Rich Skovlin investigated the area to the right of **Figure 38** and located a large can dump over the ledge that extended down to French Creek. People living in these and other buildings nearby would have used the dump as their disposal.

Figure 38. Buildings at the Southwest End of Lincoln City, Looking East, 1925. (Courtesy H.L. Turner Collection, Summit Historical Society)

Figure 39. Similar View as in Figure 38, 2000. The two buildings, now gone, would have been located to the right and behind the photographer. (Photograph by Author)

Figure 40. The West End of Lincoln City, Looking West, 1942. Note the building on the right. (Courtesy H.L. Turner Collection, Summit Historical Society)

Figure 41. Similar View as in Figure 40, 1975. (Courtesy of the Summit Historical Society)

Depression Era Mining

On October 28-29, 1929, the New York Stock Exchange crashed, wiping out 40 percent of the value of the stocks on the exchange. Many businesses closed their doors. Factories shut down. Banks failed. Farm income dropped by half. Three years later, approximately one out of every four Americans was unemployed. By 1933, the value of the stock on the Exchange amounted to less than a fifth of what it had been at its peak in 1929. The Great Depression lasted in the United States until 1939.

With so many Americans unemployed and with little hope of finding work, men turned to the gold fields of Summit County as they did in 1859 following the great depression of 1857.

Old mines re-opened. Men with gold pans, homemade rockers, and long toms lined the stream beds. Evidence of this depression-era mining still litters the ground in French Gulch. (**Figures 43, 44, 45, 46, 47, 48, 49, 50**) Discarded hydraulic pipe, sometimes cut in half lengthwise, once again transported water. Miners repaired and/or rebuilt cabins that had been abandoned for years. Bottles and cans from the 1930s littered dumps and mingled with those from the late 1800s and early 1900s.

The men lived in some of the old cabins in the area. (**Figure 37**)

The *Denver Post* in "Colorado's Golden Horseshoe," explained that those coming to Colorado hoped to make a living by opening the old mining operations. **Figure 42** shows the Golden Horseshoe that included Colorado Springs, Cripple Creek, Fairplay, Leadville, Alma, Breckenridge, Georgetown, Empire, Idaho Springs, Central City, Boulder County, and Denver.

The article included two photographs with captions: "Above—A prospector panning gold, and, center, as he appears with his pack train;" "Right—The modern miner never fails to include an armed guard in removing gold dust for shipment to the bank." (December 31, 1933)

Figure 42. Depression Era Mining in Colorado. (*Denver Post*, December 31, 1933)

Figure 43. Galvanized Bathtub and Wash Pan in French Gulch, 2002. Depression Era miners of the 1930s made use of whatever they found. (Photograph by Author)

Figure 44. Parts of a Homemade Rocker, 2002. (Photograph by Author)

Figure 45. Bed of a Wheelbarrow and Hydraulic Pipe used by Depression Era Miners, 2002. (Photograph by Author)

Figure 46. Half of a Hydraulic Pipe for Transporting Water, 2002. (Photograph by Author)

Figure 47. Riffles and Grizzly. The metal slats, called riffles, most likely lined the bottom of a wooden sluice. The perforated box, a home-made grizzly, rested on top of a rocker box. (Photograph by Author)

Figure 48. Head Gate and Hydraulic Pipe, 2002. A ditch brought water from a stream to the head gate. Depression Era miners used the water from the pipe to wash gravel into a sluice. (Photograph by Author)

Figure 49. Large Placer Operation, 1930s. Miners in the Depression Era made use of the large truck bed. This and another similar truck, about 100 feet away, can be found just west of the Country Boy mine. (Photograph by Author)

Figure 50. Placer Operation adjacent to the Mining Operation in Figure 49. (Photograph by Author)

Muriel Wolle

Muriel Sibell Wolle, who came to Colorado in 1926, taught at the University of Colorado in Boulder. Interested in the old, mostly deserted, mining towns, she visited them frequently, gathering information from locals while sketching and painting what she saw.

She wrote several books. In *Stampede to Timberline*, she tells of her visit to Lincoln City between 1938 and 1949 and the two men she met who lived in one of the cabins. They provided her with the early history and showed her some gold dust and a gold nugget they had found on nearby Farncomb Hill. **Figures 51** and **52** are from her book and used with permission.

Figure 51. Muriel Wolle's Drawing of Lincoln City with Farncomb Hill in the Background. (*Stampede to Timberline*)

Figure 52. Drawing by Muriel Wolle of Lincoln City, circa 1938-1949. (*Stampede to Timberline*)

1950s to 1990s

In the 1950s, William Bersonnet lived in the Jacot house (**Figures 46, 58**) while working at the Wellington mine. He also held the unpatented mining claim on which his house sat.

He began retrieving old cars that he parked in the trees, amassing at least 100. At that time, the Jacot house became known as the place with the old cars. Soon, a mobile home joined the cars. In 1960 or thereabouts, Bersonnet sold Slim Carol his unpatented mining claim plus all the old cars.

In the early 1970s, Slim Carol sold the unpatented claim to Floyd Hughes, who had been living in one of the buildings in Lincoln City. When Hughes moved into the Jacot house, he not only owned the unpatented mining claim, the house, and all the cars; the sale even included a bulldozer. He worked his mine near the Jacot house. (**Figure 70**)

As the cars aged, some gained value as collectables. These he restored and sold. Others, worthless, he sold as scrap.

Someone decided Hughes needed company and gave him a cat that he named Samantha. One feline became hundreds. The cost for food drained his finances. The cats took over the house and outbuildings. Eventually the smell of cat urine became so strong that people wouldn't go near him.

In 1977 or 1978, while working for Robin Theobald on a building project in Breckenridge, Hughes confessed that he actually feared the cats. By this time, Hughes lived in one of the cars because the cats had taken over the house. One day, Hughes didn't show up for work. Concerned, Theobald drove to his home. He recalls going to the back door of the house and seeing another building behind him with cats trying to escape and perhaps attack him. From that time on, Theobald believed some of the stories Hughes

Figure 53. Lincoln City, 1960s. Compare this to Figure 1. (Photograph by Robert L. Brown)

Figure 54. The Jacot House, 1962. The Jacot family lived in this house in 1916, located just east of the Jacot tunnel. (Courtesy Maureen Nicholls)

Figure 55. Cabin in Rich Gulch above Lincoln City, 1862. (Courtesy Maureen Nicholls)

told him about the cats. When Theobald spoke to Hughes, he learned that Hughes had business to conduct and failed to tell Theobald that he would not be working that day.

In the 1990s, Guy and Ruth DeMarco befriended Hughes, who was losing his sight. They helped him move to Grand Junction.

Hippies, who moved to the Breckenridge area in the late 1960s and early 1970s, refurbished the old cabins and lived in them rent free. Theobald recalls hippies in the early 1970s living in the first cabin on the right at the entrance to Lincoln City. No traces of the cabin remain.

Figure 56. Lincoln City looking East, 1975. (Courtesy of the Summit Historical Society)

Figure 57. Jacot House, the "Cat House," in Lincoln City, 1975. (Courtesy of the Summit Historical Society)

Figure 58. Buildings with Old Car, 1975. (Courtesy of the Summit Historical Society)

2001

In 2001, long after Hughes departed, Fountain visited Lincoln City to take photographs and found unlocked doors. He visited the "cat house" first. (**Figures 59, 60, 61, 62, 63**) The smell of urine remained so strong, he held his breath, took a few photos, and ran for fresh air. Cat feces covered the floor of every room.

He could not access the log building east of the "cat house," which probably dated from the 1860s. (**Figure 64**) The extension to the building on the left (**Figure 66**) and the building on the right show signs of more recent construction.

The shed in **Figure 66** dates from the early 1900s. **Figure 67** shows the inside of the shed in 2001.

Figure 59. "Cat House" and Outbuilding, 2001. (Photograph by Author)

Figure 60. Living Area in the "Cat House," 2001. (Photograph by Author)

Figure 61. Living Room in the "Cat House," 2001. (Photograph by Author)

Figure 62. Refrigerator in the Kitchen of the Jacot "Cat House," 2001. (Photograph by Author)

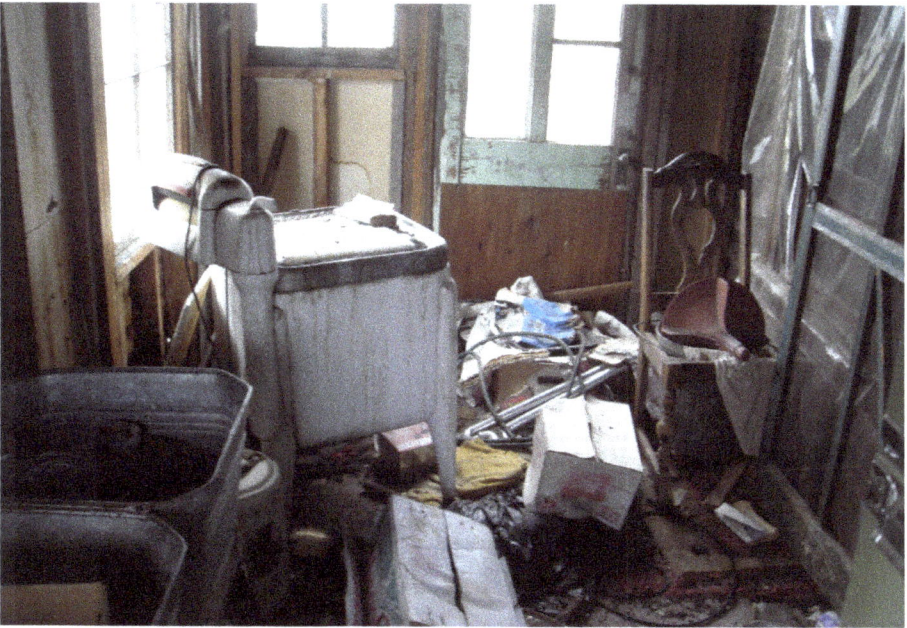

Figure 63. Laundry Room in the "Cat House," 2001. (Photograph by Author)

Figure 64. Log Building remaining in Lincoln City, 2001. (Photograph by Author)

Figure 65. Addition and Shed added to Log Cabin, 2001. (Photograph by Author)

Figure 66. Frame Building at the Eastern End of Lincoln City, 2001. (Photograph by Author)

Figure 67. Inside of the Frame Building in Figure 66, 2001. (Photograph by Author)

Hughes worked in a mine on his unpatented claim. **Figure 68** shows the remnants of the road leading to the mine.

Figure 68. Road approaching Floyd Hughes's Mine Site, 2009. (Photograph by Author)

Figure 69. Building on Mine Dump, 2009. (Photograph by Author)

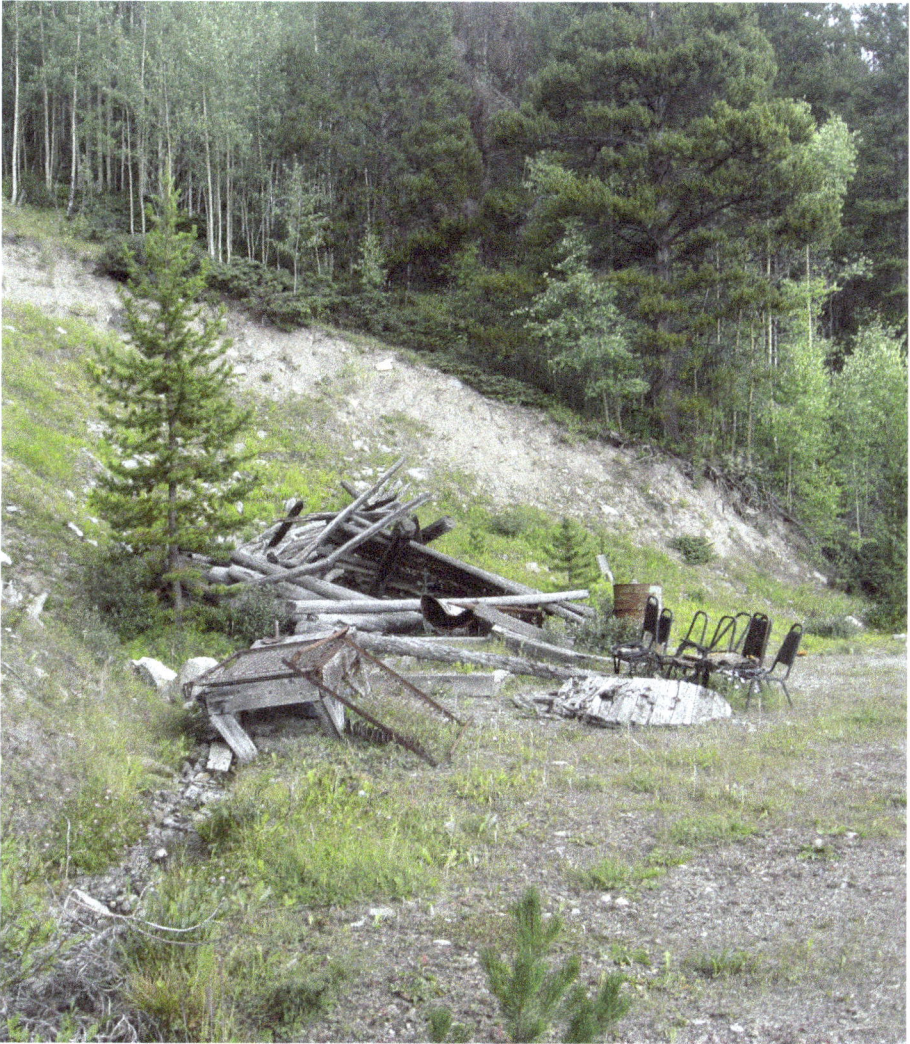

Figure 70. Collapsed Mine Adit and Dump at Hughes Mine, 2009. (Photograph by Author)

Based on Twitty's December, 2010, *Lincoln Townsite* report, the U.S. Forest Service in the summer of 2013, hired a company to remove all debris and non-historical buildings at the townsite. Workers cleaned out those buildings not destroyed, including the "cat house." Log fencing along the north side of the road separated the road from the Lincoln City site.

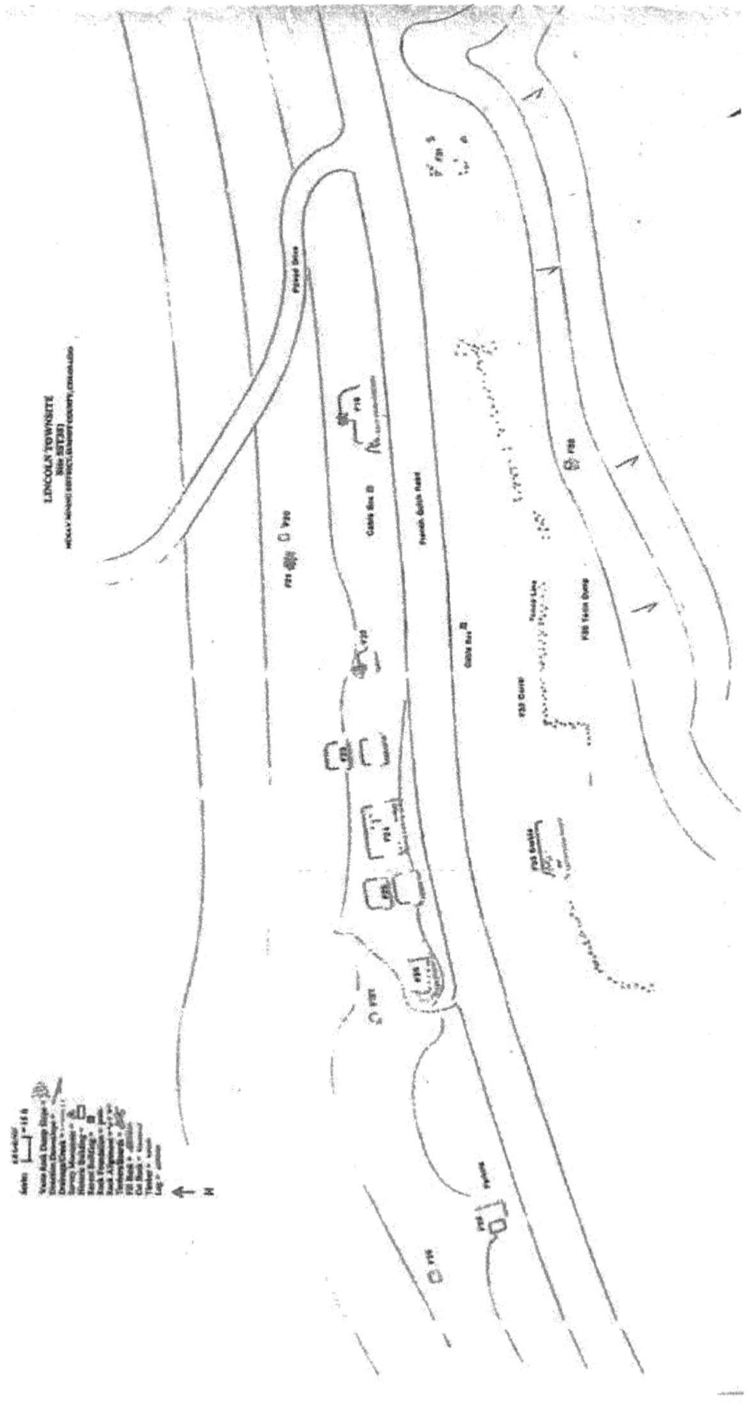

Figure 71. Twitty's Site Map of the Western End of Lincoln City. (Courtesy Mountain States Historical)

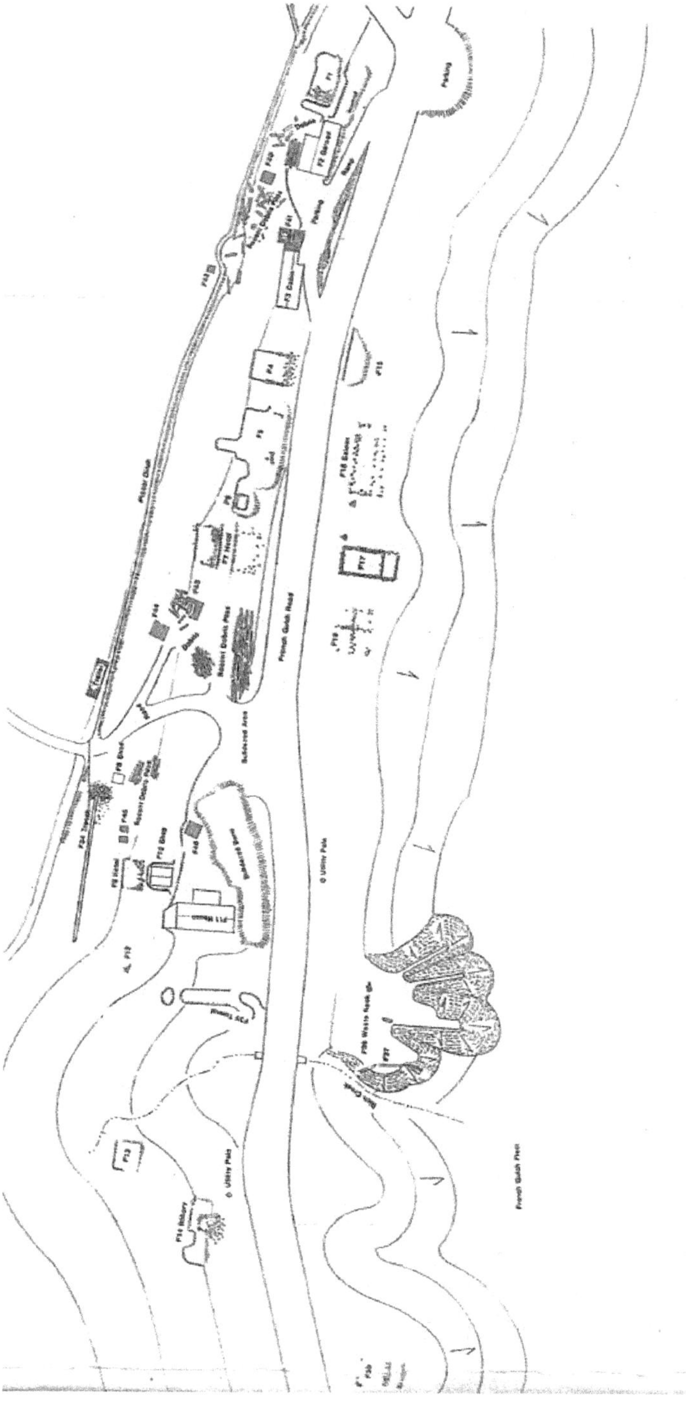

Figure 72. Twitty's Site Map of the Eastern End of Lincoln City. (Courtesy Mountain States Historical)

Fountain returns to Lincoln City every summer to photograph the buildings and surroundings. **Figures 73** and **74** show one of the true ghost towns left in Summit County.

Figure 73. The Jacot or "Cat House," 2009. (Photograph by Author)

Figure 74. The Jacot or "Cat House," 2019. (Photograph by Author)

Figure 75. Living Area inside the "Cat House," 2019. The Forest Service removed debris from the building in 2013. (Photograph by Author)

Figure 76. Another Room inside the "Cat House," 2019. (Photograph by Author)

Figure 77. Yet Another Room inside the "Cat House," 2019. (Photograph by Author)

Figure 78. Upstairs in the "Cat House," 2019. (Photograph by Author)

Figure 79. Log Cabin built in the 1860s in Lincoln City, 2019. (Photograph by Author)

Figure 80. Another View of 1860s Log Cabin, 2019. (Photograph by Author)

Figure 81. Inside the Log Cabin, 2021. (Photograph by Author)

Figure 82. Frame Building added to the East End of 1860s Log Cabin. (Photograph by Author)

Figure 83. A Frame Building East of the Log Cabin, 2021. (Photograph by Author)

Figure 84. Frame Building from the Early 1900s, 2021. This is the eastern-most building remaining in Lincoln City. (Photograph by Author)

Figure 85. Interior of Building in Figure 84, 2021. (Photograph by Author)

Figure 86. Eastern End of Lincoln City, looking West, 2021. (Photograph by Author)

Figure 87. Western End of Lincoln City, looking West, 2018. (Photograph by Author)

Figure 88. Aerial View of the Lincoln City Townsite, 2021. (Google Earth, Imagery ©2021 Maxar Technologies, U.S. Geological Survey, USDA Farm Service Agency, Map data ©2021)

BIBLIOGRAPHY

Books, Articles, and Mining District Logs

Brown, Robert L. *Colorado Ghost Towns-Past and Present.* Caldwell, Idaho: Caxton Printers, 1972.

Fountain, Bill & Mather, Sandra F. Pritchard. *Chasing the Dream, The Search for Gold in French Gulch, Breckenridge, Colorado.* Breckenridge Heritage Alliance, 2012.

Gilliland, Mary Ellen. *Summit 25th Anniversary Edition.* Alpenrose Press, 2006.

Ransome, Frederick Leslie. *Geology and Ore Deposits of the Breckenridge District, Colorado.* Professional Paper 75, Department of the Interior, U.S. Geological Survey. Washington, D.C.: Government Printing Office, 1911.

Twitty, Eric, (Mountain States Historical). *Lincoln Townsite, Summit County, Colorado, Recordation and Significance Evaluation.* Prepared for U.S. Forest Service, White River National Forest, 2010.

Wolle, Murial Sibell. *Stampede to Timberline.* Denver, Colorado: Poertner Lithographing Co., 1949.

Newspapers and Magazines

1. The website, Colorado Historic Newspapers Collection at https://www.coloradohistoricnewspapers.org

   a. *Summit County Journal*, 1891 to 1909 and 1914 to 1923, Breckenridge, Colorado
   b. *Breckenridge Bulletin*, 1899 to 1909, Breckenridge, Colorado

c. *Summit County Journal and Breckenridge Bulletin*, 1909 to 1914, Breckenridge, Colorado

d. Miscellaneous other historic Colorado newspapers

2. *Colorado Postal Historian*, Volume 16, Number 1, August, 2000

Other Sources

Bureau of Land Management, Lakewood, Colorado

Colorado School of Mines, Arthur Lakes Library, Golden, Colorado

Colorado State Archives, Denver, Colorado

Denver Public Library, Western History Section, Denver, Colorado

Summit County Clerk and Recorder's Office, Breckenridge, Colorado

Summit Historical Society Archives, Dillon, Colorado

INDEX

Bald Mountain Mining District: 28
Bella Union: 39-31, 35, 37
Bersonnet, William: 90
Bevin Mining District: 23, 24
Bissell, Judge G.G.: 23
Blair, Charles H.: 29, 48, 49
Blanchard, George A.: 63, 68-70, 72, 76
Carol, Slim: 90
Cemetery: 41-43
Clark, Calvin: 38, 48
Day, Mrs. May: 49
Depression Era Mining: 83-88
Doepke, Frederick: 38
Dyer, Father John Lewis: 32-35, 38
Eckhardt, Otto (Alto) E.: 62, 65, 68, 70
Farncomb, Harry: 59, 60, 64, 65
Foote, Robert W.: 62, 65
Ford, Barney L.: 30, 31
French Pass: 11-13, 18
Gooding, Jasper K.: 58, 60, 63, 65
Higgins, Oliver: 18
Hughes, Floyd: 90-95, 100, 101
Iliff, William: 31. 48
Langrishe & Dougherty: 36
Laurium: 73, 74
Lincoln City Hotel: 66-70
Lincoln City Quartz-Mill: 59, 67
Lincoln City Silver Company: 58, 60, 61, 66, 69
Lincoln City Smelting Works: 57
Lincoln City Stamp Mill: 66, 70
McKay Mining District: 24-27, 37
Milner, William H.: 41-43, 73

Muhlebach, Peter: 27, 35, 40
Nelson, George P.: 70
Nolan, John: 44, 47
Ontario mine: 58-60, 66-69, 77
Paige City: 16-18, 23, 28, 29
Paige, Greenleaf: 18, 22,
Paige, Prince W.: 18
Perkins, Augusta: 73
Pollock, W.P.: 31
Ripley, W.C.: 19, 21, 41, 48, 50, 53
Silverthorn, Marshal: 36, 40
Sisler, John and Catherine: 44-47
Spears, Henry: 49
Stilson Patch Mining District: 36, 37, 48
Strickler, James M.: 59, 60, 68, 69
Townsend, Albert G.: 38
Turner, James Martin: 80-82
Weber Gulch: 19, 41, 48, 50, 51, 53-55
Weber, Nate: 19, 20,
West McNulty Mining District: 23
Wilson Mining District: 38, 39
Wilson, Roland J.: 79
Wolle, Muriel Sibell: 89, 90

ABOUT THE AUTHORS

Bill Fountain

Bill Fountain grew up in Southern California where he began working in the tire business while still in high school and eventually became part-owner of 23 Big O Tires stores. He and his wife, Jeanne, moved to Denver in 1987 when he was a vice-president of Big O Tires, Inc. In 1988, he purchased several of the Big O Tires stores in the Denver metro area. Although he sold his last three tire stores in December, 2009, Bill still does some consulting for other Big O Tires dealers.

In 1988, after he and Jeanne purchased a home in Breckenridge, Bill began spending his summers investigating old cabins, mines, and ghost towns and collecting books and photos. He teams with Rich Skovlin, Maureen Nicholls, and Rick Hague exploring backcountry sites. Bill spent many hours looking through records in the Summit County Courthouse in Breckenridge; the Bureau of Land Management Archives in Lakewood; the Federal Center in Lakewood; the Colorado School of Mines, Arthur Lakes Library in Golden; History Colorado; and the Denver Public Library—as well as reading historic newspapers on the Colorado Historic Newspapers website. He has transcribed over 3,500 pages of Breckenridge mining history and has a collection of more than 3,500 digitized photographs from the 1860s to 1980s. During the summer months, Bill gives special presentations and leads tours for the Summit Historical Society, Breckenridge History (previously Breckenridge Heritage Alliance), and the Frisco Historic Park & Museum.

Bill and Jeanne traveled to Hawaii in 1969 on their honeymoon, spending time in Honolulu, Kauai, and in Kailua Kona on the Big Island. They returned several times to Kona in the 1970s and 1980s. In 1994, they purchased a time share at Kona Coast Resort, spending five weeks there each year. In 2003, they purchased a small condo; and in 2005, they upgraded to a large townhouse. In January, 2010, now fully retired, they purchased a home where they spend eight to nine months a year.

Even while in Hawaii, Bill continues his research on Breckenridge history. He and Jeanne return to their home in Highlands Ranch for the summers to be near their children and grandchildren. They rent a place in Summit County for two months each summer as Bill continues exploring the fascinating history of Summit County.

Bill has worked on special research projects for local authors, Mary Ellen Gilliland and Dr. Sandra Mather, Breckenridge History, Summit Historical Society, and the Breckenridge History Archives.

In 2014, Bill received the prestigious Theobald Award from Breckenridge History for his contributions to the preservation of Breckenridge's history.

In 2023, Bill received a lifetime membership to the Summit Historical Society.

Dr. Sandra F. Pritchard Mather

Dr. Sandra F. Pritchard Mather is a *professor emerita* in the Department of Earth and Space Sciences at West Chester University in Pennsylvania where she taught geology and meteorology before retiring in May, 1999. Since coming to Summit County in 1980 to complete her doctoral dissertation for the University of Oregon, she has written many books about the geologic, geographic, and historic landscapes of the county and those who lived here from 1859 until the turn of the century: *Southern Summit, A Geographer's Perspective; Roadside Summit, Part I, the Natural Landscape; Roadside Summit, Part II, the Human Landscape; Dillon, Denver, and the Dam; Men, Mining, and Machines; Behind Swinging Doors, the Saloons of Breckenridge and Summit County, Colorado—1859 to 1900; Golden Gulches, Hydraulic Mining in and around Breckenridge, Colorado; Summit County*, part of the Arcadia Images of America series; Frisco and the *Ten Mile Canyon*, also part of the Arcadia Images of America series; *They weren't all Prostitutes and Gamblers, the Women of Summit County from 1859 to the Turn of the Century; Historic Footprints, A Picture Book for Young Readers;* with Rick Hague, *Windows to the Past*, and with Bob Schoppe, the *Narrow-Gauge Railroads of Summit County*, part of the

Arcadia Images of Rail series. Sandie is co-author with Bill Fountain of the *Chasing the Dream* series, *Chasing the Bad Guys, Enforcing the Law in Breckenridge, Colorado, Town Marshals 1881-1923*, and *County Boy Mine, Breckenridge, Colorado, 1881-1994*.

Sandie spent summers in Summit County leading tours and presenting special programs for the Summit Historical Society, the Frisco Historic Park & Museum, and Breckenridge History. In 2013, Sandie received the prestigious Theobald Award from Breckenridge History for her contributions to the preservation of Breckenridge's history. She is a former president and life member of the Summit Historical Society.

www.ingramcontent.com/pod-product-compliance
Lightning Source LLC
Chambersburg PA
CBHW060411090426
42734CB00011B/2281